THE DECISION ROOM

A TRUE STORY OF CONFLICT, CLARITY, AND CHANGE

Avraham Lalum

The Decision Room

Copyright © 2025 Avraham Lalum

All rights reserved.

No part of this publication may be reproduced, distributed, or transmitted in any form or by any means, including photocopying, recording, or other electronic or mechanical methods, without the prior written permission of the author, except in the case of brief quotations embodied in critical reviews and certain other noncommercial uses permitted by copyright law.

ISBN: 979-8-89571-155-2

This book is a work of nonfiction based on real events. Some names, details, and circumstances have been changed to protect privacy and to serve the narrative flow.

First Edition, 2025

Published independently.

The Decision Room

A True Story of Conflict, Clarity, and Change
By Avraham Lalum
Ph.D. Researcher | Founder of Decision-Oriented Mediation

I don't enter when the deal begins.
I enter when it's already breaking.
When silence is louder than shouting.
When trust is gasping for breath.

These aren't just conflicts.
They're real stories.
Stories I've lived.
Stories I've carried.

Moments not just from the mediation room —
but from my own life.
Moments when resolution wasn't a tactic,
but a decision to stay
when walking away would have been easier.

I mediate between people.
But also between past and future.
Between power and pain.
Between the noise outside — and the truth within.

Because sometimes,
the moment you choose to mediate
is the moment you finally choose yourself.

Dear Reader,

I didn't write this book to impress you.
I wrote it to tell the truth.

The truth about what it means to shift.
To choose again.
To lead — not from above, but from within.
From the other side of a fight.

I was a lawyer. A builder. A leader.
And then, one day, I wasn't.

But what I discovered in that silence… changed everything.

This book is made of real rooms.
Real moments.
Real decisions.

It's for anyone who's tired of noise and hungry for something real —
for presence, for clarity,
for a kind of change that begins in the heart and ends in resolution.

Thank you for opening this book.
May it remind you that even when everything seems to fall apart…
something deeper may be coming together.

With gratitude,
Avraham Lalum

DEDICATION

This book was written in the space between moments —

in the quiet between questions, in the stillness that follows loss, and in the silence that asks not for answers, but for presence.

It is not a story of triumph. It is a story of returning — to what matters, to what holds, to what remains when everything else is stripped away.

I did not write it alone.

To my mother, **Tamar** — who taught me that to truly listen is to truly love.

To my wife, **Tehilee** — your steady heart has held me in every storm.

To my children, **Adam, Ari, and Ema** — you are the reason I believe in new beginnings.

To my family — your faith in me was the first quiet that gave me voice.

This book is yours as much as mine.

Thank you for helping me hear what I needed to write.

With all my heart,

Self-published by Avraham Lalum, in honor of Emma

Foreword

The Decision Room

I didn't leave the courtroom because I failed.
I left because I listened — first to others, and then, finally, to myself.

There was a moment.
One silence.
One look exchanged between two people on the edge of a costly conflict.
And in that moment, I realized something simple — and life-changing:

Conflict doesn't need to be won. It needs to be heard.

I had spent years winning cases, arguing positions, mastering legal tools.
But something was missing:
The space between the words.
The pause before the answer.
The moment where people stop fighting… and start seeing.

The moment I chose to mediate didn't happen on a stage.
It happened in a quiet room.
No audience. No applause.
Just two people — and one person willing to guide them somewhere new.

This book is a collection of those moments.
Real stories. Quiet insights.
Truths that don't live in courtrooms,
but in the spaces where people remember how to be human.

If you've ever stood in the middle of a disagreement and thought,
"There has to be another way" —
this book is for you.

Because sometimes, the most powerful thing you can do
is not to argue louder…
but to be the one who listens first.

A. Lalum

ABOUT THE AUTHOR

Avraham Lalum is an Israeli legal expert, mediator, and thought leader in real estate and cross-border dispute resolution.

With over two decades of experience in law, business, and public leadership, he has represented major real estate projects and led some of the most complex negotiations in Israel and abroad.

He served as **Deputy Head of the Israel Bar Association**, **Chairman of a Regional Cities Association**, and a **member of the Netanya City Council**, where he helped shape public policy in law and urban development.

After heading a successful law firm for 20 years, he chose to step away from litigation and dedicate his career to structured, empathetic, and decisive mediation. As the founder of the **Decision-Oriented Mediation** model, he brings clarity, presence, and professionalism to the mediation table.

He is currently completing his doctoral studies in law, lectures at leading academic institutions, and continues to mediate high-stakes commercial, family, and international disputes.

His vision is simple but profound:

To build bridges where others see walls — and to guide people not only toward agreement but toward understanding.

INTRODUCTION – PART I

The Rooms You Never See

A True Story of Conflict, Clarity, and Change

There are rooms you never see.

Moments no one records.

Decisions made in silence — between breaths, between fears, between hopes too fragile to name.

This book was born in those rooms.

It is not about grand battles fought under bright lights.

It is about the quiet battles — the ones you fight when no one is watching but everything is at stake.

Behind every contract, every negotiation, every lawsuit,

there is a human story that few ever hear.

This is a book about those stories.

The ones that happen when people reach the end of what they can fix on their own —

and must decide whether to break apart or build something new.

These are real stories.

Real rooms.

Real silences.

I did not come to this world by accident.

I walked a long road — through law, through leadership, through loss, through letting go.

I carry with me moments of triumph and moments of reckoning.

Victories measured not only in contracts signed, but in futures preserved.

My story — though you will catch glimpses of it — is not the center here.

It is simply the path that brought me close enough to witness the fragile, courageous work that happens when people choose understanding over destruction.

Each story you will read here comes from a real place,

a real room,

a real moment when everything could have gone one way —

and somehow, it went another.

You may find something of yourself here.

Not because you sit at a negotiation table,

but because, somewhere in your life,

you have stood at the edge of something breaking.

Maybe it was a business.

Maybe a relationship.

Maybe a dream.

You know what it feels like when silence weighs more than words,

when presence matters more than power,

when staying in the room is the bravest choice you can make.

That is the heart of this book.

Before we step inside, let me tell you briefly how I came to stand at these crossroads —

not to center my story,

but to honor the journey that placed me in the rooms where real decisions happen.

A Room No Longer Mine

The office was quiet.

Not the peaceful quiet of a day well spent,

but the hollow quiet of a place that no longer felt like home.

I walked through the halls slowly that evening.

Each step a memory.

Each framed certificate and photograph a reminder of years spent building not just a firm — but trust.

Twelve months earlier, I made the conscious decision to sell the firm I had built from the ground up.

It was not a decision born of defeat.

It was born of purpose.

I knew the time had come to move forward —

to begin a new chapter rooted in everything I had learned.

But I wasn't prepared to abandon what I had created.

Not overnight.

From the very beginning, it was clear:

I would stay.

Five years if necessary.

Not for profit.

Not for title.

For responsibility.

For loyalty to the clients who had entrusted me with their futures.

For loyalty to the ideals that had shaped every deal, every negotiation, and every hard-won success.

The Bridge That Couldn't Hold

At first, it felt possible.

The transition was careful, respectful.

There were moments of genuine collaboration.

But slowly — imperceptibly at first — differences emerged.

Not in method alone,

but in spirit.

Where I measured success in trust preserved,

they measured it in margins gained.

Where I valued silence and careful listening,

they favored speed and volume.

It was not malice.

It was a different compass.

And over time, it became clear that while I had planned to stay and nurture a careful bridge between what had been and what could be —

the other side had a different urgency, a different end in mind.

Promises once spoken clearly became clouded.

Commitments, once assured, began to erode —

not through overt betrayal, but through a slow, inevitable drift away from the foundations we once shared.

It hurt.

More than I admitted at the time.

Because love for what you build doesn't end when ownership changes hands.

But love without shared vision becomes a weight —

a burden no bridge can carry alone.

A Lesson Remembered

Driving home that night, as the city lights blurred across the windshield,

another presence traveled with me.

My father's presence.

A man of few words and iron discipline.

A man whose lessons were carved not in lectures,

but in the silent way he lived his life.

I remembered something he told me long ago —

during a difficult crossroads of my youth:

"If you ever find yourself needing to betray your truth just to stay —

you are not staying.

You are surrendering.

And you were not raised to surrender."

The words echoed louder that night than they had been years earlier.

Choosing the Harder Road

It would have been easy to stay.

It was easy to tell myself that compromises were inevitable.

Those dreams had to adjust to reality.

That I could close my eyes to the small fractures, if the structure still stood.

But the harder truth was this:

If I stayed,

I would slowly lose the very thing I had built.

Not the firm.

Myself.

So, I chose.

Not out of anger.

Not out of resentment.

Out of respect.

For the work.

For the people.

For the principles that had shaped my journey from the beginning.

I stepped away.

Quietly.

Deliberately.

Carrying not the firm's name —

but its spirit.

Building a Different Room

From that choice, The Decision Room was born.

Not as a reaction.

As an evolution.

A place where the silence wasn't feared,

but honored.

A space where people could face their hardest truths without losing their dignity.

Where resolution was not forced —

but forged.

Where agreements weren't settlements of defeat,

but decisions of courage.

This book is not about me.

It is about what happens when people choose to stay in the room —

even when staying is the hardest thing they can do.

It is about the decisions you never hear about.

The battles are fought without cameras or crowds.

The victories measured not in court judgments,

but in lives mended quietly behind closed doors.

Welcome to The Decision Room.

INTRODUCTION – PART II
Building a Room Where Silence Has Power

A New Fire, A New Room

The day I left the firm; I didn't step into uncertainty.

I stepped into creation.

I didn't leave with bitterness or regret.

I left with purpose — and a fierce, familiar hunger.

The same hunger I had felt twenty years earlier, when I first began.

The same fire that had pushed me to build something from nothing once before.

It was back.

And this time, it burned cleaner, sharper, without the noise of ambition or the weight of appearances.

I wasn't chasing titles.

I wasn't chasing recognition.

I was chasing the truth.

The truth of what it meant to build a place where conflict didn't have to destroy.

A place where silence could be not a void — but a power.

The Decision Room was born not from anger at what had been lost —

but from loyalty to what had been worth building all along.

The First Steps

Setting up the new office felt almost sacred.

Every chair, every wall, every detail mattered — not because of appearances,

but because of what they represented:

A commitment to presence.

A refusal to pretend.

Very quickly, cases began to arrive.

Not through marketing.

Not through loud announcements.

Simply because the work that belongs to you —

the work aligned with your deepest truth —

has a way of finding you when you are ready.

I threw myself into it with the full force of someone reborn.

Every conversation, every case, every silence held a new kind of weight.

It was as if all the noise I had left behind had sharpened my hearing.

I didn't need to speak louder.

I needed to listen deeper.

And so, I did.

The Gift of the Quiet Season

After the first wave of movement —

after the first few cases were resolved —

came something unexpected:

Stillness.

For the first time in years,

there was space between the battles.

No urgent deals to rush toward.

No background noise of a giant machine turning endlessly.

Just a quiet stretch of time,

wide enough to feel what had changed.

At first, I resisted it.

It felt unnatural — a break in rhythm.

But slowly, I understood:

This was not emptiness.

This was breathing space.

Space to honor the path I had walked.

Space to reflect — not on what was lost,

but on what had been preserved.

Space to stand fully in the truth that walking away hadn't been surrender.

It had been survival — of values, of integrity, of self.

The quiet wasn't a pause.

It was a foundation.

It was where The Decision Room truly took root —

not as a place to win,

but as a place to listen,

to decide,

to rebuild.

Why This Room Had to Exist

The more I listened to the world outside,

the clearer it became:

We had forgotten how to hold conflict without breaking each other apart.

We had learned how to fight.

How to litigate.

How to negotiate, sometimes.

But we had forgotten how to stay.

How to sit in the unbearable tension long enough for real decisions —

not pressured settlements — to emerge.

Most rooms were built to push people toward an outcome.

Few were built to give people back their power to choose.

I wasn't interested in building another negotiation table.

I wanted to build a room where silence was respected.

Where presence was more powerful than persuasion.

Where the mediator didn't dictate — but guided.

Where decisions weren't rushed — they were earned.

What Awaits in These Pages

The rooms you are about to step into through these pages are real.

The conflicts, the tensions, the moments of near-collapse — they all happened.

You won't find neat endings here.

You won't find polished heroes.

You'll find something harder — and more beautiful:

The fragile courage it takes to stay in a conversation when every instinct tells you to run.

The quiet power of choosing dignity over domination.

The slow, patient birth of solutions not manufactured — but discovered.

These stories are not about me.

They are about what can happen when people refuse to turn conflict into war.

And perhaps, somewhere along the way,

you'll recognize yourself:

In the fear.

In the silence.

In the unexpected strength that rises when you decide not to surrender —

but to build.

One room at a time.

One decision at a time.

Welcome — truly — to The Decision Room.

TABLE OF CONTENTS

11 .... Introduction – Part I

11 .... The Rooms You Never See

20 .... Introduction – Part II

20 .... Building a Room Where Silence Has Power

30 .... Chapter One

30 .... The Moment I Let Go — and Everything Began Again

49 .... Chapter Two

The Case That Changed Everything: How Decision-Oriented
49 .... Mediation Was Born

57 .... Chapter Three

57 .... When the Method Is Tested *And Not Everyone Believes*

62 .... Chapter Four

62 The Time I Chose Not to Lead: When Presence Isn't Welcome

73 .... Chapter Five

The Proposal That Came Too Early – And Nearly Ruined
73 .... Everything

84 .... Chapter Six

84 . The Mediation That Fell Apart — and Taught Me Everything

92 .... Chapter Seven

92 .... Crossing Cultures – When Words Aren't Enough

98 .... Chapter Eight

When Giving in Is Just Exhaustion And My Role Was to Stop It 98 ....— Just in Time

105 .... Chapter Nine

105 .... The Guest Who Stayed at the Center of the Table

113.. Chapter Ten

113..................................... The Refusal That Protected Everyone

120 ....Chapter Eleven

120 .... The Mediator's Dilemma

127 .... Chapter Twelve

127 .... Principles or Control?

135 .... Chapter Thirteen

135 .... Between a Decision and a Moment of Truth

145 ....Chapter Fourteen

151 ....Chapter Fifteen

151 .... The Last Light from That Balcony

157 ....Chapter Sixteen

157 .... Across Borders, Between Words

162 .... Chapter Seventeen

162 .... Beyond the Break — When Listening Replaces Litigation

167 ....Chapter Eighteen

167 .... What Wasn't Written — And What Changed Everything

171 .... Chapter Nineteen

171 .... The One Who Steps In — And Dares to Stay

179 .... Chapter Twenty

179	When the Site Stops — and the Heart Must Keep Going
187	Chapter Twenty-One
187	The Time I Said Yes
194	Chapter Twenty-Two
194	One Presence That Changed Everything
200	Chapter Twenty-Three
200	Everyone Said Yes – Then He Stood Up
207	Chapter Twenty-Four
207	The Signature That Stopped the Clock
216	Chapter Twenty-Five
216	**When I Became the Mediator**
218	**Act I: The Legal Wound That Wouldn't Close**
219	**The Mediator's Dilemma — This Time, With Skin in the Game**
220	**The Proposal: A Peace That Doesn't Heal**
221	**Speaking to the Ghosts of My Integrity**
222	**The Meeting Before the End**
223	**The Signature That Wasn't a Surrender — Yet**
225	**The Fire That Still Burns**
228	Final Chapter
228	When You Cross to the Other Side:
233	Afterword: What Comes Next
235	Decision-Oriented Mediation

CHAPTER ONE

The Moment I Let Go — and Everything Began Again

"The secret lies in timing — and in knowing what truly matters."
"Sometimes, it's not you who chooses to walk away — it's your truth that finally calls you to stop running."

That morning, there was an odd kind of silence.

Not peaceful, but the kind that emerges right before you hit the **"Undo Everything"** button.

I stood at the door of my law office —

the one I had built with my own hands,

with my own hours,

with quiet pride —

and I knew, with terrifying clarity,

this was the end.

Is there such a thing as a graceful goodbye?

Maybe — if you no longer care.

But I did.

Too much.

Even as I walked away,

even through the pain,

a part of me still wanted the firm to succeed.

To endure.

To grow.

I don't know why.

I just… did.

The scent of freshly printed paper.

The soft hum of the printer beside me.

My desk — where every item sat exactly as I liked it.

Even the morning calm I once cherished

had turned into a deafening hum beneath a truth I could no longer ignore.

I walked away.

I left behind a well-oiled machine.

A stable income.

People I trusted.

Or thought I did.

I left a legal career that had been more than a livelihood.

It had been my identity.

And the hardest part?

I left without knowing if I would ever feel at home again.

You don't lead for decades — build, fight, and create — only to crumble when the ground shakes.

Yet, even leaders, even builders, have moments when the silence around them drowns out any plan they had.

But I wasn't afraid.

Because I knew this:

Every foundation I laid — in the law, in business, in people — held meaning.

Every scar I carried had purpose.

And even this moment, this pause, wasn't the end. It was the refining of something deeper.

Some moments don't question your capability.

They question your commitment.

To the truth.

To the process.

To the quiet voice inside that whispers, "You didn't come this far by accident."

I believe in the long road.

In the integrity that comes with hard-earned wisdom.

In the clarity that follows the storm.

And I believe — not blindly, but because I've lived it —

that even when the path forward feels uncertain,

those who walk in faith… never walk alone.

A Farewell That Was Never Just a Farewell

Ilana's phone rang.

"Are you sure?" she asked, her voice barely above a whisper —

as if speaking too loudly might cause me to lose my footing.

"I'm sure," I replied.

Trying to convince her.

Trying to convince myself.

Was I certain? No.

But I was at peace.

And there's a difference.

When the place you once stood with pride

no longer feels like it honors your path —

when the desk where you once signed documents

stops reminding you of why you began —

you know.

It's time.

But this wasn't the end.

It was the beginning of a story

that had quietly been writing itself in the background of my life.

When I said I was leaving, the masks came off.

Promises vanished.

Commitments dissolved.

Agreements were denied —

as if they had never existed.

And so began the quiet unraveling of everything I thought would last.

The Fight You Didn't Choose

I wrote letters.

Drafted position papers.

Sought legal advice.

But inside, I didn't want war.

I wanted closure.

I wanted to part ways — like human beings.

But not everyone who walks your path

is willing to walk with you through the ending.

So began the legal battle.

It wasn't the kind that shocked you.

It was the kind you expect — and dread.

The kind where you find yourself justifying your humanity

through agreements once made with handshakes

but never sealed in ink.

And me?

I found myself clinging

not to the documents —

but to the version of myself

that refused to let bitterness define the future.

Because in the quiet of that rented room, I understood:

The real fight isn't about money.

It's about how you want to live the rest of your life.

I wrote letters.

Drafted position papers.

Sought legal advice.

But inside, I didn't want war.

I wanted closure.

I wanted to part ways — like human beings.

But not everyone who walks your path

is willing to walk with you through the ending.

So began the legal battle.

It wasn't the kind that shocked you.

It was the kind you expect — and dread.

The kind where you find yourself justifying your humanity

through agreements once made with handshakes

but never sealed in ink.

And me?

I found myself clinging

not to the documents —

but to the version of myself

that refused to let bitterness define the future.

Because in the quiet of that rented room, I understood:

The real fight isn't about money.

It's about how you want to live the rest of your life.

The Room Without a Name

I needed a place to work.

So I rented a small room.

No view. No espresso. No warm greetings.

Just me. A desk. A laptop.

And a black notebook I barely touched.

At first, I sat there empty.

Then angry.

And finally — open.

From that bare, silent space, a thought took root:

I'm not going back.

They thought I was walking away.

They didn't realize I was just changing form.

I didn't leave the fight.

I chose a different battlefield — one where words matter more than weapons,

and silence isn't surrender — it's strategy.

The truth is, I don't know how to stop.

I don't quit. I will recall.

When the lights go out and the room turns cold —

that's where I do my best work.

Because I don't lead for approval.

I lead because I remember what it means to rebuild from ashes.

And when you've done that once —

you stop fearing the fire.

The Stranger Who Brought Me Back to Myself

One day, a man came to see me.

Simple clothes. Tired eyes.

He asked if I was the mediator.

"I am," I said.

A few days later, he returned

and placed a brown folder on my desk.

Then he looked me in the eye and asked:

"If even you stop believing that people can change — who will?"

He wasn't talking about the dispute.

Not the other party.

He was talking about belief itself.

In people.

In healing.

In the power of a conversation not yet finished.

That night, I sat at my computer — and nearly quit.

And then, like a whisper from the past, a line returned to me:

"The quality of mercy is not strained.

It droppeth as the gentle rain from heaven..."

Shakespeare.

And suddenly I remembered:

There is power in mercy.

There is courage in letting go.

I didn't want to win.

I wanted to stop fighting.

Learning to Mediate While Still Broken

When I began to mediate, I wasn't ready.

Not emotionally.

Not professionally.

Not even financially.

But I learned — painfully and honestly —

that being a mediator isn't about being neutral.

It's about being human.

Knowing when to speak.

When to listen.

When to hold the silence,

even when you're the one unraveling.

Oz

Oz walked in with a fierce at his side.

He barely spoke.

At one point, he turned to me and asked:

"Do you honestly believe this has a chance?"

I didn't answer immediately.

Just met his eyes.

Then said:

"I don't know if it does. But I know this — you're not alone."

That moment changed everything.

Because sometimes, more than a solution,

what a person truly needs —

is to feel seen.

The Choice to Stay

There were days I considered going back.

Law firms. Tempting offers.

But I knew —

returning would cost me something greater than money.

It would cost me… myself.

And that's when I understood the real secret:

I never left the law.

I simply stepped into it from the other side.

Not from the side of power —

but from the side of presence.

Then, People Came

I didn't market.

Didn't advertise.

But people came.

People with tired eyes.

People with broken hopes.

People who weren't looking to win —

but to breathe again.

They didn't want revenge.

They wanted a chance.

I wasn't there to replace the lawyer in me.

I was there to remind him

why he existed in the first place.

And Out of Silence, a Method Was Born

Not academic.

Not theoretical.

But practical.

Rooted in people.

Decision-oriented — and heart-driven.

I wasn't perfect.

But I was real.

Present.

Committed.

Wounded.

Human.

Romania

Then came the call from Romania.

A tangled dispute between Israeli and local partners

in a crumbling development project.

The flight was instinct.

The situation — chaos.

I didn't know the language.

Didn't know the customs.

Just the silence on the other end of the phone.

I arrived in an old boardroom.

One side raged.

The other shut down.

The architect quit.

I stayed.

Not to fix —

but to listen.

And slowly, something softened.

A Hebrew word.

An awkward handshake.

A coffee break in a too-small kitchen.

And there —

trust returned.

It wasn't a contract that changed things.

It was the feeling that someone had come

not to win — but to understand.

Not to represent one side —

but the possibility

that this could end differently.

Now

Now, I stand on the other side.

I understand the fracture.

The suspicion.

The fear.

The silence.

And because I understand it —

I know how to lead.

Not from above.

From beside.

And maybe that's the real secret:

Not every ending is a failure.

Sometimes, it's a quiet invitation to begin again.

We hold onto what's familiar —

titles, roles, definitions we've built or been given.

But sometimes, when everything slips away —

a new door appears.

You don't always see it right away.

But it's there.

Life doesn't always ask for permission.

Sometimes it just pushes.

And in the space between what you've lost

and what's waiting —

you meet a truer version of yourself.

Not the one who wins.

The one who chooses to believe again.

Because only after you've truly let go —

can you finally understand why you had to.

And when you look back,

you see what you couldn't at the time:

Every chapter had a reason.

Every fall had its purpose.

And the moment you thought you were breaking —

was the moment you began to become whole.

CHAPTER TWO

The Case That Changed Everything: How Decision-Oriented Mediation Was Born
A Cliff Without a Net

It happened sooner than I expected. When I chose to leave my law firm behind, I imagined a pause — a breath, a moment to rebuild. But life doesn't wait for you to be ready, especially not when the world around you is already breaking.

I hadn't opened an office. I didn't have a team or a practice. I wasn't yet anyone's mediator — just someone who had stepped off a familiar cliff, hoping something new would catch him.

Then the phone rang.

"If you don't come," the voice said, "it's over."

Not a request. Not a plea. A verdict.

A Room Held by Silence

That morning, I stepped into a borrowed office space on a high floor downtown. Neutral. Unfamiliar. And full of silence. It had been waiting there even before the first person arrived.

Floor-to-ceiling windows framed the city, and a long wooden table stretched across the room. The light was sharp, like truth. The air was thick with dread.

The project was collapsing — a large-scale urban renewal was unraveling.

I said nothing. I let them sit.

The lawyer for the tenants isolated himself in a corner. The developer checked his watch like it owed him something. The binder on the table, packed with contracts, signatures, and timelines, remained untouched.

It wasn't just a legal crisis. It was emotional. Personal. Like a broken family dinner, where no one knows who still belongs.

"I want a moment," I said. "No talking. Just... wait with me."

Breaking the Silence

Silence deepened, until a voice from the tenant's side whispered:

"He doesn't really represent us. Not anymore."

No one objected. No defense. The sentence landed like something overdue.

And suddenly, I understood: This wasn't about mediation. This was about holding the room together.

They didn't need a method. They needed someone who would stay when everything else fell.

So, I stayed. I didn't speak like a lawyer. I didn't facilitate. I sat beside them. I listened. I asked not what they signed — but what was whispered, promised, left unwritten.

They hadn't come to negotiate. They had come to grieve.

The tenants felt abandoned. The developer was terrified — not just of losing the deal, but of losing the years, reputation, and trust invested.

Drawing a New Path

And me? I had come to listen, but I was standing at the center of a human fracture — something traditional mediation could not hold.

If I asked how they felt, they would retreat. If I remained neutral, they'd see weakness.

So, I offered something else: a path. Keep the current attorney temporarily. Appoint a second, tenant-chosen representative. Biweekly meetings. Full document access. External advisor — advisor jointly agreed. Three months. Review. Decision.

Then I stopped. And let the silence take over.

The Grounded Beginning

I didn't come into that room as a strategist or technician. I came in with my head grounded, my heart open, and my hand steady on the wheel. Not to dazzle. Not to impress. But to stand — to hold — until they could find their footing again.

That's when I understood: true mediation isn't about cleverness or manipulation. It's about presence. It's about staying still when everything around you wants to collapse.

The Birth of Decision-Oriented Mediation

Decision-Oriented Mediation wasn't born from theory. It was born from necessity — the need to act, not just observe. To know when to let silence stretch and when to offer a bridge. To understand that neutrality doesn't mean standing aside — it means standing firmly in the center, without tipping the balance.

Every choice I made that day — to listen deeper, to offer structure without control — became the first brick in a method built for real people, in real crisis.

The Three Pillars of the Method

Over time, the method shaped itself around three living principles:

1. **Clarity over complexity**: No jargon. No hidden agendas. Just the truth, spoken clearly and bravely.
2. **Presence over performance**: It's not about how you sound. It's about what you hold — for yourself, and for others.
3. **Movement over stagnation**: Even when no agreement is reached, good mediation always creates movement — forward, inward, human.

These pillars weren't invented. They discovered one human fracture at a time.

Leading Without Losing Yourself

Leadership in the Decision Room isn't about commanding authority. It's about carrying trust — even when it's fragile, even when it's unspoken.

It's about holding onto your center, your ground, your quiet strength, while storms rage around you. The method asks not: *"How do I win this room?"* It asks: *"How do I keep this room from breaking?"*

And sometimes, the bravest thing a mediator can do is not to find the perfect words — but to simply stay.

A Moment That Held

First, nothing. Then questions. Then — something shifted.

They began to speak. Not to me. To each other.

It was hesitant. Broken. Real.

That was the moment. The moment Decision-Oriented Mediation was truly born.

Not from books. Not from theory. But from a fracture. From failure. From human weight.

What Remained

That night, I stayed after they left. Chairs empty. A coffee cup half-full and cold. And a room still holding something it hadn't in weeks — possibility.

I didn't solve it. But I didn't let it break.

And that was enough.

But something deeper stayed with me that night. Not the solution — but the ache. Because I helped mend someone else's crisis, I was still standing in mine.

I didn't speak about it. Didn't share it. But I carried it — every step of the way.

Because here's what most people never see: You walk into that room and give everything. Focus. Strength. Patience. You guide people through chaos while carrying your own.

And when the room empties, when the hands are shaken and the silence returns — you're still in it. Still holding.

Choosing How to Fight

But that doesn't make you weak. It makes you real.

Because leadership isn't about having no wounds. It's about walking with them — and still standing.

That's when I understood: Mediation isn't where you escape the battle. It's where you choose how to fight it.

You don't lead by detaching. You lead by anchoring. By knowing that even as you help others rise — you never let go of your own ground.

From that day forward, I never asked clients what they wanted. I asked what they were ready to carry.

Because the strongest voice in the room is not always the loudest. It's the one that holds — even when it's not heard.

And sometimes, the most powerful thing a mediator can do is not to reflect, or reframe — but to stand still, and not let the moment break.

Beyond the Moment

And maybe that's what this book has been about all along. Not just telling the story of what mediation is — but living it, page by page.

In the rooms where silence screamed. Where trust had to be rebuilt word by word. Where clarity rose not from calm, but from collapse.

Because when you choose to mediate — to truly mediate — you're not stepping away from conflict. You're walking right into it.

Not to dominate. Not to disappear. But to be present. Decisive. Human.

And if even one person, one story, one moment in these pages reminded you of that — then perhaps it did what it came to do.

And just as one moment ends, another begins. The method was born. Now, it had to be tested. (Transition to Chapter Three)

CHAPTER THREE

When the Method Is Tested *And Not Everyone Believes*

The Door Before the Storm

It didn't begin with a warning letter. It began with a door.

A door I had stood before many times before — but this time, it felt different. The weight of what waited behind it wasn't just procedural. It was personal.

Three days earlier, I had received the letter. Official. Ice-cold. Measured down to the last comma. A senior law firm declared that I had no authority — that my proposals would be tolerated but never accepted. Reviewed, but never honored. Reduced to commentary.

But long before the letter — before the table, the folders, and the chairs — came the doubt. That familiar voice every innovator knows: "They won't accept you." "This won't work." "You don't belong here."

I heard it. And I walked through the door anyway.

A Room Designed for Battle

The room was sterile, curated like a battlefield. Glass table. Cold light. Color-coded folders laid out in formation. Faces carved in caution.

But beneath the strategy, something older lingered: Fatigue. Of being stuck. Of pretending this was still about documents. Of knowing that another failure might finally break it all.

I didn't enter with a defense. I didn't sell my model. I offered one thing:

"Let's see if there's anything still here worth saving."

That line did something. Just enough. My muscles eased. A breath held was released.

The First Offer

Then came my first proposal: A thread. A beginning. Not a demand.

The lead attorney challenged me immediately. "This isn't protocol."

I nodded. "And neither is this situation."

Then came the slow unraveling of control. Not chaos, but surrendering rigidity.

A recalibration.

I offered structure: Timelines.

- Shared checkpoints.

- Accountability without ego.

- A pause before the plunge.

They didn't welcome it. But they didn't walk away. And sometimes, staying in is the boldest decision a room can make.

The Weight of Doubt

That night, I walked back to my apartment in silence. No music. No calls. Just the echo of that room in my chest.

Was I forcing something? Were they just tolerating me?

I sat at my desk and opened the same notebook I had used when designing the method. I flipped to a blank page and wrote one line:

"The real test of a model is not in how it is introduced, but in what it survives."

And at that moment, I knew: This wasn't about winning them over. It was about withstanding the moment they didn't believe.

A Shift in Ownership

The next day, something shifted. They questioned less. They adjusted more. Not because they accepted the model, but because they began to own it.

Three days later, they signed. No smiles. No satisfaction. Just a breath — finally exhaled.

As one of them passed me through the door, he muttered: "Thanks... for staying."

That line. That moment. That presence was the true beginning of this method.

The Power of Presence

And since then, every room I enter echoes that scene. Every resistance reminds me: People don't need perfection. They need someone who will not run.

That is what makes Decision-Oriented Mediation real. Not brilliance. Not theory. But presence.

Because the one who stays shifts the whole room.

Toward the Next Room

And just as one test ends... another door waits. Another table. Another silence. Another chance to hold the room when no one else will.

And I will be there.

CHAPTER FOUR

The Time I Chose Not to Lead: When Presence Isn't Welcome

A Room Not Ready

It began with a silence I could feel before the first word was spoken.

Not the kind of silence that opens a conversation — the kind that shuts it down before it starts.

Late arrivals. Barely concealed eye rolls. A stiffness in posture that said, "We don't want to be here."

Two former partners, now bitter opponents, accompanied by legal counsel, armed with documents, timelines, and grievances.

They weren't here for mediation. They were here because the court said they had to try it.

They didn't greet me. They nodded — because they had to.

And so, I did what I always do: I listened.

But what I heard wasn't what was being said. It was what was underneath.

The Room That Refused to Breathe

They couldn't agree on anything.

Not on the timeline.

Not on the facts.

Not even on what their original contract had said.

There was a version of me — a younger version —

That would have stepped in.

Offered options. Named patterns. Suggested frameworks.

But I didn't.

Because somewhere between the lines and the looks, I realized:

They weren't here to reconcile.

They were here to prove the other wrong.

And so, I said less.

At one point, one of them looked at me and said, "He's probably already drafted a proposal. That's what they do."

I smiled.

"Not this time," I replied.

That was the first moment they looked at me with anything other than resistance.

"Why not?" the other asked.

"Because there's no draft to work from.

Because you haven't finished speaking yet — not really."

The Power in What I Didn't Say

It wasn't hesitation. It was discipline.

I had ideas. Structures. Tools. Precedents.

But the most responsible thing I could do was nothing.

Because not every silence demands movement.

Not every mediation demands direction.

Sometimes, the room just isn't ready.

And when it's not, pushing it forward doesn't help.

It breaks it.

Another Room. The Same Stillness

That same month, I was handling a different case.

A man came into my office one autumn afternoon —

quiet, worn down, eyes heavy with the kind of tiredness that has nothing to do with sleep.

He sat down gently, almost cautiously.

And said: "I'm not trying to hurt him. I just want him to finish the work or give me the money back. That's all."

No contract dispute. No legal theory.

Just an unfinished apartment.

Exposed walls. A kitchen that didn't exist.

A pregnant wife. A baby on the way.

No shower. No sink. No peace.

He had paid for everything up front. Because he believed.

And when that belief was betrayed, he didn't call a lawyer.

He asked for mediation.

He wasn't looking for compensation.

He was looking for dignity.

For completion.

For quiet.

A Wall of Deflection

The contractor came in with a very different energy.

Experienced. Confident. Guarded.

He brought a "technical advisor," who did most of the talking —

deflecting, interrupting, and reframing everything in his favor.

They weren't looking for a solution.

They were looking for signal control.

Every answer was a slogan.

Every question — a trap.

And the man across the table — the one who had been left behind — began to shrink.

I tried everything.

Separate sessions. Gentle reframing.

Moments of quiet. Even humor.

But the table wasn't open.

The Sentence That Shifted Everything

Then, during one of the quieter private meetings, the contractor finally broke character.

Just one sentence. Softly: "I need to keep my name clean. I have two more projects pending."

And there, a door opened.

Not legally. Humanly.

Not in anger. In worry.

Not a Proposal — A Possibility

I didn't offer a solution.

I offered a starting point.

Not a contract — but a draft.

Not a position — but a possibility.

The client, the one who had waited through silence and deflection, asked for two things: Correction.

And a signed commitment.

The contractor agreed.

Not with joy.

But with understanding.

With necessity.

And the case ended.

Not in harmony — but in honesty.

When Doing Less Is Leading More

I learned more from those two cases than from any textbook on mediation.

Not about techniques.

About restraint.

The discipline is not to solve.

The wisdom not to offer.

Because sometimes, what a room needs most —

is someone who doesn't rush in to fix it.

Sometimes, it needs someone who stays… even when there's nothing to say.

The Myth of Movement

We live in a world that praises motion.

That sees progress in updates, drafts, changes, and steps.

But real progress isn't always loud.

And momentum isn't always moving.

Sometimes, the most powerful act is waiting.

Sometimes, it's holding space for people to catch up with themselves.

Sometimes, it's knowing that your role isn't to lead them forward —

But to keep them from falling further behind.

The Shift You Don't See

One of those partners called me weeks later.

He didn't say much. Just that he had been thinking.

The next day, the other one did the same.

No signatures yet.

No resolutions.

But something had changed.

Because someone, for once, hadn't tried to push them.

Because someone had simply stayed.

The Wisdom in Stillness

I didn't lead that day because there was nothing yet to lead.

And because I respected them enough to wait.

That, I believe, is mediation.

Not making people agree.

But staying long enough for them to make space for themselves.

When No Map Exists

There is a difference between offering direction and forcing a path.

There is a difference between silence that confuses and silence that invites.

I don't always know which is which.

But I know what it feels like when the room isn't ready.

And I know how to stay.

What's Left When No One Wins

Those two cases didn't end in triumph.

They ended up doing something better: Understanding. A quiet kind.

A tentative kind.

But understanding, nonetheless.

You Stay. That's the Story.

Not every conflict ends in agreement.

Not every session ends with a handshake.

Not every proposal needs to be written.

Sometimes, the most human thing you can do —

is to recognize what isn't ready — and not try to force it open.

Sometimes, you stay.

And that is enough.

What Comes Next

And then… sometimes the one who stayed becomes the only one they're willing to call again. Because when the next case comes — and it always does — they remember who didn't leave.

CHAPTER FIVE

The Proposal That Came Too Early – And Nearly Ruined Everything

A Draft on the Table. A Shift in the Room.

There are moments that never leave you.

Like the quiet tension in the room the moment I gently placed the mediator's proposal between two former business partners.

Two men who had built something together —

an investment firm, a legacy, perhaps even a kind of brotherhood.

Now, they were ready to part ways — or at least trying to.

Not with hostility.

Not with noise.

But with the kind of sadness that follows when something once full of life becomes too heavy to carry.

They didn't hate each other.

But they couldn't speak to each other, either.

So, they came to mediation —

not to fight, but to separate without destruction.

We Just Need a Way Out

From the start, I felt the tension.

Not anger, but emotional fatigue.

Two people sitting across from each other, accompanied by lawyers.

Each had told me the same thing, separately:

"Please… help us find a way out.

Don't let this become a mess."

So, we began.

We mapped out the assets.

Reviewed the legal structures.

Discussed risk, responsibility, and contributions.

There was progress —

not fast, but real.

Like a small boat carefully navigating away from a storm.

The Draft I Thought Would Help

And then — maybe out of hope, maybe out of fatigue —

I decided.

I wrote a proposal.

A short, structured document.

Clear assumptions.

Defined steps.

Not a verdict — just a direction.

And I laid it gently between them.

They looked at it.

And then everything changed.

Silence.

A long, dense, sinking silence.

Then one of them said:

"There it is.

Exactly what I was afraid of.

A proposal that looks good on paper — but doesn't see me."

The other didn't speak.

But he leaned back,

not in agreement, but in disappointment.

Or maybe fear.

The eye contact vanished.

Their postures stiffened.

And the fragile trust we had built?

It fractured.

Not loudly —

but completely.

When the Proposal Becomes the Problem

There is a fine line between guidance and intrusion.

In decision-oriented mediation, a proposal is a legitimate tool —

but only if delivered at the right moment.

Not just the right content —

the right rhythm.

A proposal must arrive in sync with the room —

as a natural progression, not a shortcut.

That evening, I learned that lesson firsthand.

I hadn't proposed too early.

I had done so before they were emotionally ready to be seen.

It wasn't the content that failed.

It was the timing.

I Took a Step Back

I didn't explain.

I didn't defend the document.

I simply said:

"I hear you.

Maybe I jumped ahead.

Let's take a step back."

And we did.

Not Numbers — But Wounds

We returned to separate sessions.

We stopped discussing figures and started discussing feelings.

Not about percentages —

but pain.

Not about balance sheets —

but about the experience of letting go.

They weren't asking for a solution.

They needed space.

Not silence as escape —

but silence as acknowledgment.

The kind of silence that says:

"I'm here, even now."

A New Language Emerges

We started sketching.

Flowcharts.

Diagrams.

Not to win —

but to understand.

We developed a new language.

Not one of positions —

but of questions.

Eventually, we held a private meeting — without the attorneys.

And there, I finally heard their unfiltered voices.

They spoke of betrayal.

Of fatigue.

Of the loneliness that comes when a partnership stops feeling mutual.

The Second Proposal Wasn't a Proposal

Later, I sent a new document.

It wasn't a solution.

It was a skeleton.

No numbers.

Just structure.

A shape they could mold.

They didn't accept it.

But they didn't reject it either.

They revised it.

Questioned it.

Made it their own.

When Silence Holds More Than Words

When trust began to return —

when silence became readiness —

I offered a third version.

It didn't resemble the first.

It wasn't clinical.

It breathed.

It had space for doubt.

Room for pause.

Lines like:

"This is a possible direction.

Let's explore it together."

And this time —

it landed.

A Proposal Isn't a Verdict

A mediator's proposal isn't a conclusion.

It's opening.

It doesn't end a conflict —

it invites its transformation.

It doesn't always succeed —

but when it's timely, it's remembered.

It becomes a compass point.

The Most Important Lesson

That case taught me something I carry into every room:

Don't propose because you can.

Propose because it's time.

And sometimes —

the most powerful proposal is the one you don't make.

The draft you keep in your folder —

because the people in the room aren't ready to receive it —

that's the proposal that honors the process.

To Propose is to Listen

Now, whenever I write a mediator's proposal,

I think back to that moment:

The man who said,

"This doesn't see me."

And I try —

before drafting anything —

to see.

Not just the logic.

The humanity.

Not just the claims.

The cost.

Because a mediator's proposal is not a solution.

It is an act of recognition.

It says:

"I see the shape of what might be.

Do you want to build it together?"

It is not a verdict.

It is a bridge.

One step at a time. With room to breathe.

CHAPTER SIX

The Mediation That Fell Apart — and Taught Me Everything

When Mediation Ends Without Agreement – But Opens a Door to Something Else

Not every mediation ends in resolution.

And not every failure is truly a failure.

Some cases don't result in signatures but still change you forever. This is the story of one such case. A process that didn't deliver a formal agreement but revealed something deeper: not all solutions are written on paper. Sometimes, failure isn't the end — it's simply one station along the path.

A Morning That Felt Too Perfect

I remember the day vividly. Not because something dramatic happened, but because nothing happened. There were no raised voices. No slammed doors. Just silence. The kind of silence that settles in your bones. Not external. Internal.

That morning, everything seemed to align. The coffee was just right. The room was warm. The staff was on point. Everything looked ready. But inside, I knew this one would be different.

A Decade Together — Then the Drift

They were seasoned partners.

Not just colleagues — more like brothers.

Together, they'd built a successful urban planning consultancy.

One was the strategist — meticulous, numbers-driven.

The other was the connector — passionate, grounded, all intuition and relationships.

Over a decade, they built a reputation. A portfolio. A team.

And then — No collapse.

No betrayal.

No scandal.

Just... wear.

Vision drifted.

Energy faded.

Resentment brewed silently.

One felt the other always took the credit.

The other felt alone — like the weight of the firm rested on him.

Eventually, they agreed:

It was time to part.

The First Meeting – A Room of Ice

They arrived right on time.

Dark suits. Cold stares.

They sat across from each other as if they hadn't once shared not only an office — but a purpose.

"We're here to see if there's anything left to salvage," one of them said.
"We're not here for hugs."

The other said nothing.

Not out of defiance.

Out of restraint. The kind of restraint that hides a wound.

We started the process.

Session after session.

Draft after draft.

Emails. Legal notes. Attempts.

There were even moments of dry humor —

Fragmented memories of better days.

I could still see a thread between them.

Thin, but present.

But the closer we came to resolution —

The further apart they drifted.

Each Draft Collapsed

Every version we shaped —
Every set of terms —
Broke down.

Paragraphs became minefields. Then one day, during a coffee break, the moment arrived.

"It's Not Just Me"

They had left the room separately.
I was sitting alone with one of them.

Maybe it was fatigue.
Maybe it was the right pause in the day.

He looked at me and said:

"It's not just me.
I'm not the only one in this."

He paused. Then added:

"There's someone I owe.
Just as much as he owes me.
If I sign something he hasn't seen…
I'll be repeating the same mistake my family made years ago."

I didn't understand it right away.
But in the days that followed, the picture sharpened.

The Person Not in the Room

It wasn't a lawyer.
Not a silent investor.

It was his older brother. A seasoned businessman who had once experienced a failed partnership of his own.

He wasn't in the room — but he was controlling the pace.
Not to dominate — but to protect.

Except his protection had become a blockade. Every time we approached agreement, that brother's shadow pulled it back.

"I'm Not Going Any Further"

We came close.
So close. One party had agreed.
The other went silent for a week. Then another.

Then he returned. "I'm not going any further," he said.
"The other side isn't being honest."

Everything fell apart. No shouting.
No confrontation.
Just silence.
Again.
And this time, it stayed.

An Unexpected Call

Two weeks later, my phone rang.
Unknown number.

"Hi… this is Yoav. I'm his brother. I think we should meet."

There was something in his voice — not regret. Not defense.
Curiosity.

We met in a quiet café, far from the glass towers and legal papers.
He ordered mint tea. I had black coffee.

And for two hours — we talked.

Not about equity splits. Not about deadlines or project managers. But about fear. About trust. About how his own experience shaped, how he advised his brother.

"I saw him heading into the same disaster I went through," he said. "I didn't want him to be alone in the wreckage."

I asked him "And what if he wasn't heading into disaster? What if he was heading toward closure?"

Yoav blinked. "Then maybe I stopped him from healing."

At that moment something cracked open. And it wasn't about fault. It was about weight.

The burden of past trauma — passed down like a legacy.

Healing Doesn't Always Happen in the Room

The case didn't end in a signed agreement. There were no headlines. No handshakes.

But weeks later — I heard through someone on the team: They'd started speaking again. Emails turned into calls. Calls into meetings.

Eventually — they decided to restructure the company, not dissolve it. Not to keep things as they were — but to build something new, from the ashes.

The Lesson That Changed Me

Some mediations don't give you a trophy.
They don't end with photos or applause.

But they leave you with truth. With humility. With the reminder that what's visible in the room — is never a full story.

And sometimes, it's not the document that changes everything —
It's the conversation that happens after the silence.

That case taught me that failure is never final. It's just another version of unfinished.

And unfinished stories — can still have beautiful endings.

CHAPTER SEVEN

Crossing Cultures – When Words Aren't Enough

The Mediation That Began in the Sky – and Taught Me to Listen Differently

The flight was scheduled, but nothing prepared me for the storm that awaited above — or inside.

It wasn't the turbulence outside that shook me. It was the one within.

I sat by the window. Outside, darkness. Inside, a faint light. And beside me, two strangers — completely silent — mirroring exactly what lay ahead: two people in conflict who didn't share a language, yet had no choice but to understand each other, or crash.

This wasn't my first cross-border mediation. But something about it felt different.

Maybe it was the fact that I had just launched my new firm. Maybe it was the quiet pressure of needing this to work. Maybe it was the feeling that the table waiting for me wasn't only covered in documents — but layered in emotion, memory, and culture.

When Culture Isn't a Clause — It's a Way of Life

Two partners.

An Israeli entrepreneur — dynamic, intuitive, hands-on, allergic to bureaucracy.

A European counterpart — meticulous, process-oriented, formal.

They had signed a partnership agreement, established a company, and moved forward with a residential development. For months, everything went smoothly.

And then — the details began to break apart:

Who approves the budget? How are the planning changes decided? When can costs be offset?

The Israeli said: "We talked about this. You know what we meant."

The European replied: "If it's not written — it doesn't exist."

As tensions grew, they turned to their lawyers. And then — they paused.

Because neither of them wanted war. They just didn't understand what had happened.

Starting Without the Contract

On day one, we didn't discuss the documents.

We didn't talk about money.

We talked about trust.

"What does partnership mean to you?" I asked.

"How do you recognize trust when it's there?"

Their answers weren't just different — they were opposites.

The Israeli spoke of intuition, moving fast, and adjusting as needed. Trust, for him, was built by doing.

The European spoke of structure, clarity, and written agreements. Trust, for him, was built by boundaries.

So, I had to translate.

Not just language — but mindset.

Not just words — but roots.

The Proposal Was a Translation, not a Compromise

For five days, we built a plan.

It wasn't a compromise — it was a translation.

We took what the Israeli wanted to "lock in fast" and wrapped it in oversight: a neutral accountant, a clear approval process.

We took what the European demanded "in detail" and broke it into staged implementations.

The plan included:

- A gradual exit from the joint company

- Regulatory oversight by a local advisor

- Involvement of a neutral accountant

- System coordination checkpoints

- A revised disclosure package to the bank

Every line was translated. Every concept was clarified. Not just between languages — but between worldviews.

One Phone Call. One Fear.

On the fifth night, at 10:40 PM, I received a call.

It was the Israeli entrepreneur.

"Avi," he said, "I'm not sure. This feels too formal. Like I'm losing control."

We spoke for nearly an hour.

Not about clauses — but about fears.

We spoke about how, in Israeli culture, informality isn't negligence — it's flexibility. And how, in European culture, order isn't control — it's safety.

He paused.

Then said:

"If you believe this will hold us together — I'm in."

The next morning — they signed.

A Quiet Sentence Before Boarding

At the airport, just before my return flight, the client waited near the gate.

He didn't say much.

Just this:

"I didn't think it would work.

You didn't just translate words — you translated me."

What It Taught Me

Culture is an invisible contract.

Just because you understand the words — doesn't mean you understand what they mean.

Mutual respect begins with emotional translation — not just linguistic clarity.

Cross-cultural mediation requires not only expertise — but the courage to ask what hasn't been said.

The best solution is the one built in a shared new language.

This wasn't just another case. It was a turning point. Not in how to mediate — but in why.

Because in a world where agreements are written in many languages — the real resolution is written in shared understanding.

And that's when I learned:

Even when I don't understand everything — I know how to listen.

And sometimes, that's all that matters.

CHAPTER EIGHT

When Giving in Is Just Exhaustion And My Role Was to Stop It — Just in Time

They walked into the mediation room after months of legal warfare.

Two former friends. Two business partners. Two men who had once built something together — and now stood on opposite sides of its collapse.

One of them, Yossi, looked especially drained.

He slumped into the chair across from Gadi, his former partner, who spoke with sharp clarity and unmistakable command.

At one point, Yossi said quietly:

"Just give him what he wants. Let's just be done with it."

As a mediator, I've heard those words more than once.

Sometimes, they mark a breakthrough — a real willingness to resolve. And sometimes, they're a whisper of something else entirely.

Fatigue. Resignation. Collapse.

A Friendship That Turned into Friction

Yossi and Gadi founded a private real estate investment firm.

Yossi managed project development. Gadi raised capital, led investor relations, and crafted the firm's public image.

For years, they worked in harmony.

But over time, cracks emerged.

Disagreements on roles. Conflicts over recognition.

When one European project suffered losses, the spiral began.

Gadi blamed Yossi for planning failures.

Yossi claimed Gadi made reckless promises to investors.

The partnership soured.

The company froze.

Litigation – The First Attempt

Gadi filed a lawsuit to dissolve the partnership.

Yossi counter-sued.

Lawyers on both sides escalated tensions. Threats of financial damages.

Letters laced with legal venom.

Investor relations suffered.

Legal bills piled up.

Finally, someone suggested:

Try mediation.

Not just to settle — but to salvage whatever dignity remains.

The Mediation Room — One Alert, One Absent

From the first session, the difference started.

Gadi was alert. Focused.

He brought numbers, charts, legal briefs.

Yossi… barely spoke.

When asked direct questions, he gave short answers.

He didn't engage.

He didn't push back.

He didn't defend.

Not because he agreed — but because he had given up.

Gadi's Offer — And the Silence That Followed

Gadi made an offer:

He'd retain most of the firm's assets.

Yossi would exist without his full equity.

In return, Yossi would waive future claims.

On the surface — a tough but realistic deal.

But in the room — it felt like surrender. Not a resolution. Not peace.

Just… capitulation.

The Mediator's Dilemma — When to Pause a Settlement

In decision-oriented mediation, we aim for clarity and closure. But we also carry responsibility:

Never push an agreement that won't last.

Because what feels like resolution today —

can become tomorrow's regret.

Or worse — a reopened legal wound.

So, I asked to pause the session.

A Quiet Question Behind Closed Doors

In a private session with Yossi, I asked him gently:

"If you felt strong right now — would you sign this?"

He looked away. Then said:

"No.

But I don't have the energy to fight anymore."

That was all I needed to hear.

Not Pushing Forward — But Stepping Back to Protect

I recommended a 24-hour break.

Gadi was annoyed — but agreed.

The next day, Yossi returned — with a second attorney. Not to attack.

Just to steady the ground beneath him.

He asked for one adjustment:

Clearer language around the waiver.

One clause revised — to reflect a more balanced exit.

Gadi initially resisted.

But after a one-on-one conversation with me, he relented.

He understood: A fragile agreement would break.

But a firm one — built on readiness — might hold.

Resolution — Not from Collapse, but from Clarity

Two days later, they signed.

The partnership dissolved.

Assets were divided.

No headlines. No court. Just an ending that held its weight.

A month later, Yossi sent me a short email:

"Thank you n for not letting me give up on myself."

What I Learned — And What I Now Look For

Fatigue is not a foundation.

It may look like agreement — but it's just silence in disguise.

As mediators, we don't only listen to words.

We listen to where they come from.

Sometimes, resolution means stopping everything — to ask a single quiet question:

Are you saying this because it's right — or because you're too tired to say anything else?

When exhaustion speaks, we stay awake.

We hold the light.

Not for us.

But for the person who can't hold it anymore.

That's when mediation becomes more than a method.

It becomes presence.

And that, sometimes, is the difference between giving in — and letting go.

CHAPTER NINE

The Guest Who Stayed at the Center of the Table

When the Mediator Is No Longer an Observer – But Becomes the Heart of the Room

I sat across from them.

Two brothers. Two stories. One property — never formally divided.

I wore a suit without a tie. Casual. Comfortable. A quiet smile. But inside, I held one essential truth:

I was a guest.

I didn't know the family.

I didn't carry their history.

I didn't understand the layers they walked in with.

And maybe — just maybe — that's why I had a chance.

Listening Before Acting

I didn't intervene. Not immediately.

I listened.

I watched what was said — and what wasn't.

Who was reacting, not speaking? Who was holding on to old anger, and who was simply afraid to lose one more thing?

After the third session, one of them smiled — for the first time.

That's when I knew: I was no longer a stranger.

Not because I knew everything. But because they allowed me in, for a moment, into the emotional terrain where the real conflict lived.

Only then did I place something on the table. Not a solution — an invitation. Not a decree — a possibility.

The Mediator as a Guest Who's Invited to Stay

In decision-oriented mediation, you don't come to simply observe.

You enter. You watch. You wait. You lean in.

Not as a judge.

Not as an authority.

But as the one person in the room who carries no weight from the past.

And in that neutrality lies your invitation.

You are the guest in a loaded room. A room filled with broken words, silent glances, and tired hearts.

And at some point, you must act. Not to deliver justice, but to create space for understanding.

I'm often asked: "How do you know when it's time to offer a proposal?"

My answer:

When the silence stops working.

When eyes turn toward you, not with blame, but with hope.

When they ask — even without words — "What do you think?"

That's the moment.

That's when you pick up a pencil.

Draw a small line on a blank page. And say, "Let me show you something."

From Guest to Host – Without Force

You don't impose a solution.

You invite it.

You don't dictate justice.

You create a safe enough space for truth to emerge.

Your power doesn't come from authority. It comes from trust.

And when trust builds, language changes. People who once shouted — begin to search for middle ground.

Not because of you.

But because of themselves.

Still, you were the one who rearranged the chairs. Cleared the table. Laid out the map.

How to Do That Without Losing Legitimacy

You learn to walk the line between silence and suggestion.

You ask:

"Would it be helpful if I offered a thought?"

You never push.

You never assume.

Your offer with humility:

"Would you allow me to reflect on something I'm sensing?"

You choose words that open, not close. And in doing so, you build your credibility not with volume, but with presence.

And Then — Something Changes

They begin to speak differently. Not with agreements.

But with less resistance. Not about blame.

But about options.

That's when you realize:

You've become part of the room. Not as a decision-maker. But as the person who made decisions possible.

A Story That Clarifies It All

During a mediation between brothers in a family inheritance case,

it was clear from the first session:

The real battle wasn't about assets.

It was about something far older.

So, I listened.

Only after hearing the same childhood story — repeated from both sides —

Did I ask one question?

"If you could go back to that moment, what would you do differently?"

They didn't answer at first. But something shifted.

For the first time, they were not looking backward. They were looking forward.

That was the moment I became more than a guest. I became someone they trusted enough to let stay.

Other Moments from the Field

In cross-border mediation between partners from different cultures, I found myself mediating between languages, not just interests.

Even the word "responsibility" carried different tones.

So, I asked them to imagine their business as their child. What would each of them need to feel safe in it?

That question wasn't legal.

It was emotional.

And it opened a door.

The Role That Demands Humility

There are sessions where you don't need to be brilliant. You need to be quiet.

Not because you have nothing to say —

But because the room isn't ready to hear it.

You learn to wait. You learn to release your need to "be important."

So, the process—not the person—becomes meaningful.

The Mediator as Witness

Not every mediation ends in an agreement. But every mediation that creates a space for calm — is a beginning.

And the mediator?

They are the witnesses.

Silent. Present.

Not fused with the story —

But not distant from it either.

Not erasing pain.

But not letting pain write the ending alone.

You are the living reminder that another path is possible.

You are not a guest anymore.

You are part of the room.

And sometimes, you're the only light left in it.

CHAPTER TEN

The Refusal That Protected Everyone

Not Every Door Deserves to Be Opened — When Mediation Isn't the Right Path

They entered the room with frozen faces. Not in anger, but something deeper. A kind of cold mask people wear when they're too tired to even be mad.

It was a harsh winter day.

Rain outside.

Heavy air inside.

A collective real estate investment abroad had gone horribly wrong.

Four investors sat before me — former friends, and some family. All claimed they were misled.

Sold a dream.

And left with nothing.

No contracts.

No securities.

No answers.

And worst of all, no property.

It was an "investment in trust" — in someone they once knew. A handshake. A history.

Now: just heartbreak.

Facing the Void

On the other side of the table sat a representative of the development company.

Cool. Calculated. Dismissive.

He hadn't brought the promised documents.

He kept repeating: "Everything was based on mutual trust."

During a break, one investor leaned toward me and whispered:

"How can you mediate with someone who won't even say where the money went?"

I didn't answer. Not because I didn't know —

But because I understood:

Sometimes, the very existence of a mediation table creates the illusion that there's something worth negotiating.

When the Documents Don't Tell the Story

The process didn't move forward — it stalled.

And slowly, the signs accumulated:

Contradictions in versions.

Evasive answers.

Legal representatives who never appeared.

A persistent sense that something was being hidden.

Then came the moment I won't forget.

One investor, with tearful eyes, asked me:

"Do you really think he came here to solve anything?

Or just to delay the lawsuit?"

That's when I understood:

I wasn't here to find just a solution.

I was here to assess intent.

And without intention, there is no conversation. Only performance.

A Moment Outside the Process

Just as this case reached its lowest point —

I received an unexpected call from a childhood friend.

He said:

"I know you're a mediator... but what do you do when your father and brother haven't spoken in five years — and you're stuck in the middle?"

He wasn't looking for a professional solution.

He wanted comfort.

To understand how he, of all people, ended up being the go-between.

"I'm not a mediator like you," he said, "I just wanted peace at home."

That line stayed with me.

Back to the Room — Where Peace Had No Place

The next day, I returned to the mediation.

I saw the investors tired and defeated.

I saw the representative wearing that same cold smile.

And I knew:

They weren't seeking the same thing.

Some had come to resolve.

Some to survive.

And one — to hide.

When Dialogue Is Just a Disguise

I asked them to pause the process.

Not from anger. From respect.

Respect for those who came in good faith. Respect for those who deserved better than a staged negotiation.

"When a party hides information, shifts stories, and rejects transparency, mediation becomes a shelter, not a solution."

Eventually, the case returned to court.

A clear, decisive rule followed, and slowly, trust was restored.

Emotional Barriers in Other Cases

This wasn't limited to business.

In one of my most emotionally intense mediations —

A divorced couple tried to establish contact with their son.

The mother sat silent.

The father exploded in bursts of rage.

There was no shared language. Only pain. Only shame.

At one point, the mother looked at me and said:

"I don't want peace. I just don't want him to forget what he did."

I closed my notebook. Sometimes, silence is wiser than false hope.

Knowing When to Walk Away

In decision-oriented mediation, courage isn't just about proposing solutions. It's about knowing when not to.

Sometimes the story is bigger than the process. Sometimes, a bridge between two cliffs is just a mirage.

This isn't a weakness. It's leadership.

To end before damage deepens —

To pause before the table becomes a stage of harm —

That's professional judgment.

The Brave Choice to Refuse

"Knowing when not to mediate isn't a mediator's failure —

It's a victory of discernment."

From the hardest cases, I've learned:

The art of mediation isn't only about resolving.

It's about recognizing when there's no one truly to resolve with.

When good faith is absent. When words are masks. When agreement would be fiction.

That's the wisdom I carry into every room.

Not every door deserves to be opened.

And sometimes, the one that stays closed —

It is the one that protects everyone.

But then there are the times when you don't leave the room —

Yet something in your breaks.

And what happens…

When your fracture is yours?

CHAPTER ELEVEN

The Mediator's Dilemma

What Happens When You're the One Who Breaks Inside

What happens when the mediator — the one meant to hold space, embody calm, and guide others — begins to break?

This is a personal chapter.

Not about a case I resolved.

But about a moment that shattered my professional distance — and quietly changed the way I see my role.

It happened years ago, in a small room.

Average coffee.

A heavy silence.

An Old Mediation. A Quiet Collapse.

It was before my current method — before I even knew what "decision-oriented mediation" meant.

I was invited to assist in a joint mediation.

My colleague led the session — a man I respected deeply. I was there to observe, support, maybe offer balance.

The couple we met were calm.

Not young. Not loud.

But the silence between them shook the table.

They didn't shout. They didn't interrupt. They simply placed a quiet mountain of pain between them.

Not a legal dispute — a life's worth of missed signals. Regret.

Distance.

Disconnection.

A Sentence That Broke Something in Me

Then it happened.

Mid-discussion, the man turned to her and said, in a voice as cold as marble:

"You didn't hear me then.

And you don't hear me now.

You were never there."

She didn't respond. She didn't defend. She just looked at him — and something in her look felt… familiar. Too familiar.

Something inside me shifted. My shoulders dropped. My breath changed.

I couldn't explain it — but I wasn't in the room anymore.

Memory Overwhelms Technique

The rest of the session blurred.

The techniques.

The structure.

The reflective questions.

None of them mattered.

Because of that sentence?

It echoed somewhere I hadn't visited in years.

A memory.

Of another relationship. Of feeling unheard.

Of trying — and failing — to reach someone you once trusted.

It wasn't the same story.

But the emotional map was identical.

And suddenly, I wasn't the mediator. I was the one who needed mediation.

What Do You Do When You Break — in Front of Them?

I didn't know whether to speak.

Or to leave.

I didn't want to disrupt the process. But I also couldn't pretend.

Then — she noticed.

She looked away from her partner. Looked at me. And said, gently:

"I'm sorry… but are you okay?"

It shattered me.

Because in seeing me — I had to see myself.

The Turning Point of Vulnerability

I answered quietly:

"It touched something in me.

More than I expected.

But I'm here.

I'm with you.

And I'm listening."

No plan.

No theory.

Just truth.

And something opened. In her. In him. In the room.

The Process Didn't End — It Deepened

No agreement was signed that day.

But they came back.

Three more times.

And eventually — they reached a decision.

Not because I was strong. But because I had let myself be human.

The Lesson I Still Carry

That day taught me:

Neutrality is not a wall. It's a space. A flexible, living space.

And authenticity —

when used with care — doesn't harm the process.

It deepens it.

Today, when I sat across from strangers,

I remembered her look. That one question:

"Are you okay?"

And I remember the power of staying.

Of not hiding. Of letting the silence do its work.

Where Trust Is Truly Built

In that moment, I wasn't a facilitator. I was part of the human fabric in the room.

And that — more than any technique — built trust.

"The moment I almost broke…

was the moment trust became real."

Sometimes we need to tremble —

to remember what truly holds us.

And from that trembling —

clarity often emerges.

In the next chapter, we'll enter a family dispute where the principles masked a deeper pain — and uncover how naming the hurt can sometimes be the path to healing.

CHAPTER TWELVE

Principles or Control?

When a Family Property Dispute Hides a Quiet Plea for Recognition

"It's not about the money — it's about the principle."

Danny said it the moment he sat down.

No one had asked him anything yet.

He wasn't angry.

He was precise. Composed. Tense.

Pressed suit.

Stack of documents at his side.

And the voice of someone who had already made up his mind.

His three siblings — Mira, Shay, and Eyal — seemed different.

Not tense, just exhausted.

Like they'd been walking in circles for months.

The House with the Lemon Tree

A small house in central Israel.

Single-story.

A lemon tree in the backyard.

And an old bench by the entrance — untouched for over a decade.

Their parents lived there for fifty years.

The mother passed away a year ago.

Since then — only Danny remained.

"We want to sell," Mira said. "It's not that we mind him living there. It's just… it's been too long. We can't hold this shared property forever."

But Danny wouldn't budge.

"This isn't real estate," he said. "This is legacy. History."

It sounded like a cliché.

But not every cliché is empty.

A Different Case. A Mirror Image.

At the time, I was also working on a different family dispute.

Two brothers.

A family business.

A fight over who would get the back storage unit.

It seemed trivial.

But it wasn't about the space.

The older brother had spent his entire career there — not out of love, but because it was where their father had sat.

He just wanted to keep sitting in that chair. To feel like something — anything — was continuing.

Danny's Silence Was Speaking

Back in Danny's mediation, something didn't add up.

If it was just principle — why wouldn't he buy them out at a fair value? If it was only values — why reject every compromise that included him?

At our second meeting, something shifted.

Danny came alone.

No lawyer.

No files.

He sat down and said quietly:

"I haven't slept in weeks."

That surprised me.

This man — always composed.

A former lawyer.

Now a fund manager.

Suddenly — vulnerable.

"She Forgot My Name."

"You know what it's like," he said, "to bathe your mother when she forgets who you are?"

"You know what it's like to sit with her at night when she asks for Dad — and he's been dead seven years?"

I didn't respond.

He didn't want a response.

"I took care of her. Alone. For six years. My siblings were busy. I'm not angry. Not really. But this house… it's not just walls. It's me."

A Bench, A Plaque, A Memory

I thought of a woman I'd once met during a lecture.

She was fifty, divorced, and all three of her children had moved to the U.S.

I asked her why she hadn't left her small apartment.

She said:

"In that kitchen, my mother told me — once — that she was proud of me.

If I sell it… those words disappear too."

People hold on — not to places, but to anchors.

To the last thing that keeps them whole.

The Real Battle

I turned to Danny and asked:

"If the house were to be sold — what's one thing you'd want to remain?"

He paused.

Then answered:

"The bench," he said.

"A plaque. Their names. In the garden."

It hit me then — he wasn't fighting the deal.

He was fighting the erasure.

He wanted to be seen.

The Third Meeting — And the Crack That Opened

Shay — the most impulsive — exploded:

"You're selfish, Danny. You're holding us hostage. This isn't yours alone!"

For the first time, Danny raised his voice:

"And where were you when I was bathing her, Shay?

When I wiped her.

When I protected her dignity.

She forgot my name — and smiled when she remembered.

And you? You were in Barcelona."

Mira cried.

Eyal whispered, "Danny… we didn't know.

We truly didn't."

Suddenly — the numbers, the deadlines, the valuations — they all faded.

A Resolution from the Heart

We offered a solution:

– Danny would stay for one more year.

– He'd have six months to buy them out at a fair market rate.

– If he couldn't — the house would be sold.

– Each sibling would write him a personal letter.

– And in the garden — a bench.

With their parents' names. And, quietly, his own.

This wasn't a real estate deal.

This was an emotional pact.

That night, I wrote in my mediation notebook:

"Sometimes 'principle' is just pain that has no other name."

Behind the Curtain of Control

Now, every time someone says:

"It's not about the money — it's the principle,"

I pause.

Not to re-check the math. But to ask: What is it they're afraid to lose?

Because when pain speaks the language of control — sometimes the only path forward is to name what no one wants to say.

CHAPTER THIRTEEN

Between a Decision and a Moment of Truth

A meeting that never made it into the minutes — and a quiet longing for my father.

There was silence.

Not the kind that screams to be broken.

Not tension.

But something else.

Cold.

Professional.

Too professional.

Three people in the room.

Two parties in a five-million-shekel business dispute.

And me — the mediator.

No shouting.

No slammed doors.

Just a silence that started in the body — and took over the room.

And in that stillness, I knew:

If I didn't act now — it would explode.

Not because they didn't want an agreement.

They did. Badly.

But sometimes, the more people want resolution —

The more afraid they become to reach for it.

That's where I come in.

But then something happened.

Something that never made it into the minutes.

Between the first session and the second —

I lost my father.

Between Two Tables — One in Mediation, One at Home

My father wasn't a mediator.

He was a foreman.

He built houses. Fixed things. Held them up.

But he taught me something I use every day:

Never fear the moment when someone goes silent.

Don't rush to fill it.

Let it do its work.

When I got the call about his condition —

I stopped the process.

Not as a professional choice.

My body simply refused to go on.

I told the parties: we paused.

Yair sent condolences by message.

Nadav called.

He didn't talk about mediation.

He just asked: "Are you okay?"

I didn't know it then —

But that call would change everything.

Back in the Room — But Not the Same Room

Session two.

Same table.

Different atmosphere.

Yair's tone was softer.

Nadav quieter.

And for the first time —

They didn't start with legal terms.

They asked:

"How was your week?"

Something cracked open.

Not much.

But enough to let the air back in.

What I Learned from Death — and Took Back into Mediation

At my father's funeral,

A man stood beside me I hadn't seen in years.

A contractor. Someone who worked with him long ago.

He didn't come out of obligation.

He came because, as he said:

"He never raised his voice — even when a wall collapsed.

He used to say:

You fix walls.

You don't break people."

I thought about that as I sat again between Yair and Nadav.

As they argued figures.

As they tried to be right.

I thought back further —

To the summer after sixth grade.

One day, I showed up late to his construction site.

Dusty. Hot. Embarrassed.

He didn't scold.

Just handed me a hammer and said:

"Start with this beam.

You don't have to finish.

Just start."

So, I Asked Them

They were stuck.

Digging into the past.

Blaming.

Repeating what couldn't be changed.

So, I asked:

"If you had to start over —

Without the history. Without the anger —

What would you do differently?"

Not what the other should have done.

You.

Yair was silent.

Nadav fiddled with a pen.

Then spoke:

"I would've just talked to him.

Not let my lawyer speak for me."

For the first time —

He said it in his own voice.

Not through a proxy.

A Sentence from a Funeral — That Came Back in Mediation

"He never raised his voice — even when a wall collapsed.

He said: Walls you can fix.

People, you don't break."

They were both right.

And both hurting.

Sometimes people don't know how to say:

"You hurt me."

So instead they say:

"You broke the contract."

The Moment of Decision — That Started with a Pause

I offered them a break.

Separately.

Nadav stood to leave.

But Yair said:

"Can we stay here a moment — all three of us?"

Silence again.

Then:

"I don't know if we can fix this," Yair said.

"But I don't want to part ways as if we were never friends."

Nadav looked at him.

Then at me.

Then said:

"Neither do I.

But I don't know how."

That Was Enough

Not for a full agreement.

Not for reunion.

But for a different kind of conversation to begin.

A Quiet Signature — and a Bench in My Memory

They didn't go back into business.

But they closed with dignity.

They split assets.

Set boundaries.

Agreed to operational separation.

In the final session, as they signed,

Nadav leaned in and whispered:

"I hope your father will be proud of you."

I almost couldn't respond.

Just smiled. Too much.

But Some Days — There's No Time for Silence

Some cases don't leave time for space.

For process.

Everything is urgent.

Everyone's under pressure.

And in those moments —

The mediator must decide.

Not when he's ready —

But when they need it most.

Next chapter: When listening isn't enough. When pressure closes in. When you must choose to lead — or risk the collapse.

CHAPTER FOURTEEN

When No One Has Time to Feel *And You're the One Who Has to Decide*

A true story of fast-track arbitration in a high-stakes real estate project, where I was called upon to decide — quickly, sharply, and without room for maneuver. It's also a story about a stone I didn't throw as a child, and how that quiet, forgotten moment taught me how to hold space in a mediation room, even when everything is on fire.

Thursday, 9:13 PM — The Call That Left No Choice

I hadn't planned to work that evening. But when I saw the developer's lawyer on the screen, I picked it up.

"The tenants want to change representation. Their lawyer refuses. The bank's threatening to pull funding if there's no resolution by Sunday."

"Just decide," he said. "Make the call."

I stepped outside to the pool. I often do that — not to see my reflection, but to see if I'm calm. If the water is still, maybe I am too.

It wasn't.

And then, from nowhere, a memory surfaced: me, as a kid, holding a stone. The boy across from me had smashed the headlamp on my bike.

But I didn't throw it.

The Stone I Didn't Throw

That summer afternoon, the street was quiet. The damage was real. I held the stone.

One second. One decision.

But I lowered my hand.

Later, I told my father.

"Did you throw it back?" he asked.

"No," I said.

He didn't say much. Just smiled.

I think I knew, even then: sometimes, the real decision isn't what you do. It's what you don't do.

Back to the Project — And a Room That Couldn't Wait

By Sunday at 8:00 AM, the room was full: developer, lawyers, tenant committee, and me.

This wasn't mediation. This was arbitration. A decision had to be made — fast.

I told them: "Accelerated arbitration. Fourteen days. No zigzags. No spin."

They agreed. When pressure builds, someone must hold the handle.

A Fracture, Fear, and a Plea

Mrs. S., an 83-year-old resident, stood and said: "I just want to know this won't all fall apart. I don't understand everything — but I can't start over."

It wasn't about the lawyer.

It was about trust. Who would hold their fear?

And me? I just needed to remember how not to throw the stone.

A Three-Stage Resolution

This wasn't a solution written in a contract. It came from silences, hesitations, and handshakes that hoped to last.

The decision took the form of three simple, precise steps:

1. Legal representation would transition within five business days, with full documentation and transfer of materials.

2. The outgoing attorney would provide a signed commitment to cooperate professionally and maintain project continuity.

3. A 90-day standstill clause, barring either side from unilateral actions that could jeopardize the project.

They accepted.

No cheers. No celebration.

But they signed.

The Light at the Edge of the Roof

Afterward, I stepped to the side of the old building, near where the workers took their breaks.

I reached for my phone to silence notifications.

Instead, I looked up.

The sunlight caught the corner of the roof — right at the spot the tenants had feared would crumble.

When No One Feels, Someone Must

Once they left, I sat alone with the signed papers.

Everything was documented. Legal. Settled.

But something else had finished too.

Because I hadn't just resolved a conflict.

I had stood between two frightened sides, each afraid that yielding meant losing everything.

And I had held that space without shattering it.

That night, I walked again to the pool.

A ritual.

Not for answers.

Just to see myself reflected.

The water was still.

Not perfect. But still.

And I thought of that boy, with the shattered bike light and the stone in his hand.

And I told myself: the strongest decisions are often made in silence.

Not by striking back.

But by choosing to hold.

Because not every stone needs to be thrown.

And sometimes, placing it gently on the ground —

It is the loudest decision of all.

CHAPTER FIFTEEN

The Last Light from That Balcony

On Mediation, Belonging, and the Man Who Stood Between a Contract and a Fading Sunbeam

Sometimes, just when everything seems perfectly aligned, one voice — quiet, not demanding — halts the entire mechanism. This chapter revisits the story of one man, among dozens of residents in a major urban renewal project, who asked for just one thing: not to feel invisible. He wasn't aggressive. He simply couldn't bear to lose the last ray of sunlight that still entered through his balcony.

This is a story of attentive mediation, of light and legacy, and of how a mediator — who thought he had seen it all — learned to see again through another person's window. Because in real estate, as in life, everything depends on perspective.

The Phone Call That Changed the Equation

It came in the middle of a workday. A representative from a major real estate company called me, his voice tight, nearly apologetic.

"We've got 23 out of 24 signatures. One resident is refusing. And he's not extorting. He just... doesn't want to feel invisible."

And with that, I stepped into one of the most quietly human cases of my career.

This wasn't about money. It wasn't about ego. It was about light.

The Shadow Cast by Towers

The project was a classic teardown-and-rebuild under Israel's TAMA 38 frameworks. Three floors. A 1960s building. The plan was clean: new units, better infrastructure, added value. Every tenant had legal advice, access to planning documents, models, appraisals. Everything advanced quickly.

Except one unit.

Apartment 2. A long-time resident. Reserved. Respectful. Not hostile. Just... still.

He finally spoke:

"I won't sign if my sun disappears."

It wasn't a demand. It was a quiet line in the sand. And hundreds of thousands of shekels worth of planning rested on a single patch of light.

One Against Twenty-Three

Tensions boiled on all sides.

The developer? Furious. "I've worked on this for two years. I won't let one man collapse it all."

The other residents? Mixed. Some angry. Some pleading.

And the man himself? Silent. Until he said:

"Nobody ever asked how I feel."

That line stopped the room.

Remembering My Father's Sukkah

As the process unfolded, I remembered something small: my father's sukkah.

Every year, he built it just so a specific beam of sunlight would enter through a corner.

When someone trimmed the tree once, he said, "Some things you don't notice unless you're there year after year."

That resident wasn't resisting a contract. He was resisting erasure.

From Blueprint to Understanding

In our first meeting, he barely spoke. Near the end, he whispered:

"If someone had asked me seriously, I might have signed up a long time ago."

That moment shifted everything. The mediation wasn't about design anymore. It was about recognition.

Three Layers of Resolution

1) **Architectural adjustment:** A subtle shift in penthouse placement restored some daylight.
2) **Apartment upgrade:** Improved ventilation, insulation, and small refinements.
3) **A personal letter:** A signed note from the developer promising transparency.

He didn't want more square meters. He wanted to remain visible.

The Moment the Room Breathed Again

In a private follow-up, I asked: "What would make you feel that you haven't been erased?"

He paused. Then said quietly:

"If you move that wall, I'll see sunlight again. That's all I need."

And that was everything.

The developer nodded. The engineer said, "We can do that."

He signed. Not because we pressured him. Because we saw him.

Back to the Water

That evening, I sat by the pool. The same place I go when I need silence.

I looked at the water, then up at the sky.

Not to reflect. Just to breathe.

And I thought about how many times in life we cling to something not because it's the most important — but because it's the last thing that's still ours.

That resident didn't want a penthouse. He wanted to know he still existed.

When Seeing Is Everything

Sometimes people don't need more. They need to be seen.

And that's the heart of Directed Mediation: Not to push people to surrender, but to make sure they know they're still part of the picture.

Among rights, regulations, and plans, sometimes all it takes is a single ray of light to feel at home again.

Through his window, I learned to look farther. Not just across the street. But across the world.

CHAPTER SIXTEEN

Across Borders, Between Words

How a Homegrown Mediation Method Bridged an International Divide

What brings a mediator from Israel into the heart of a commercial dispute in a foreign country, in a language he doesn't speak? Not just confidence, but a method. This is the story of a case that unfolded far from home, where the Israeli approach — direct, structured, and emotionally attuned — helped reconcile parties who had long stopped believing in dialogue. This wasn't a classroom simulation or theoretical exercise. It was professionalism that assumed responsibility. And results.

For years, I mediated without calling it mediation. I guided people through hard decisions, negotiated broken trust, and lived by a rule that never failed me: don't fear silence, and don't flinch when truth knocks.

But when I left everything — the firm, the title, the reputation — and chose to build something from scratch, I realized I hadn't just developed a style. I found a method. Directed Mediation.

And this method, shaped in Israel, translated surprisingly well to places where the only language spoken is English.

The Method Was Always There — I Just Needed to Name It

Leaving the prestigious firm I had built over two decades wasn't an escape. It was a call. I didn't walk away from power — I walked toward purpose.

I wasn't coming from the shadows. I came from marble tables and cross-border deals. But I wanted more than polished outcomes. I wanted human ones.

At first, silence. My inbox stayed quiet. My doubts grew louder.

Then — a breakthrough. A fractured couple. A broken deal. Resolved in one day.

Not celebrated. But real.

The next morning: a phone call.

"I heard about you," the man said. "They say you don't just listen. You lead."

Reputation Earned, Not Marketed

He didn't find me through ads or glossy bios. He'd heard of me through real work — the kind that left handshakes, not headlines.

Deals in Eastern Europe. Agreements born out of risk. Partnerships that needed repair.

When the local mediator failed — too procedural, too polite — they wanted someone real.

Someone who knew how to manage a collapse.

A Quiet Reminder Before Departure

The day I flew out, my wife sent me a photo.

Our son, then twelve, was standing beside a crooked wall we'd fixed one summer.

I'd told him: "Buildings — like people — don't always stand straight. But you don't knock them down. You realign. Gently."

I carried those words with me. Especially this time.

Dinner Without Suits — and With Truths

The night before formalities began, a consultant from one of the teams invited everyone to dinner. Casual. Local food. No suits. Just people.

I hesitated. But his sincerity convinced me.

We sat around a crowded wooden table. Miscommunications turned into laughter. After the third drink — confessions.

That dinner didn't solve the dispute. But it melted something. It humanized the process.

Next day: same people. Different tone.

Three Days to Shift a Story

1. **Day One:** Separate talks. Cold civility. Legal positions.
2. **Day Two:** Ten hours in one room. Simulation. Real talk. No posturing.

I didn't demand agreement. I demanded clarity.

What if this fails? Who loses? What future will die?

Slowly, the conversation shifted from accusation to accountability.

3. **Day Three:** A signed memorandum. Simple. Clear. Human.

Back at the Window — and Forward in the Mission

That night, I sat at the hotel window. Rain streaked the glass. A warm room behind me. A signed agreement glows on my laptop.

And I thought: methods matter.

Not theories. Not titles. Methods.

Especially when they cross borders — not just geographically, but emotionally.

A dream born in Israel. Realized when two strangers shook hands in a foreign boardroom.

I was there. I led.

I am moving forward now. But never without echoing the path that brought me.

The method works. Not because I invented it, but because I lived it.

CHAPTER SEVENTEEN

Beyond the Break — When Listening Replaces Litigation

How a Damaged Industrial Deal Sparked a Cross-Cultural Resolution

Sometimes, when the industrial table breaks, you need to build a new one entirely — one you can sit around and speak from the heart. This chapter tells the untold story of a broken deal between an Israeli telecom executive and a European factory owner. A shipment was damaged, responsibility deflected, and trust evaporated. But then — both sides stopped. Not to surrender, but to listen. Directed Mediation entered not to mediate politely, but to lead with clarity. This is a story about cross-border silence, broken contracts, and the moment a new dialogue was born.

The Call That Crossed Continents

Four years ago, I was deep into a successful legal career. My name was known. My clients were powerful. But mediation? That word hadn't yet found its place in my professional language.

Still, the method — the heart of Directed Mediation — was already in me.

Then one evening, just back from a business trip, my phone rang. The voice on the line belonged to the CEO of a major Israeli telecom company:

"We're in the middle of a complicated deal with a factory in Eastern Europe. The local council is overwhelmed. We need someone who speaks people, not just contracts."

Thirty-six hours later, I was on a plane.

Dinner Before Documents

Rain met me on arrival. It was neither cold nor warm, just soft. Like a whisper across the stone streets. That night, by surprise, I was invited to a local dinner. A round wooden table. No suits. No folders. Just people.

Across the table: Daniel, the sharp Israeli executive. Alexei, the worn, deliberate factory owner. Tension at first. Then food. Then drinks. Then… something softened.

No agreements were made that night. But the air shifted.

Remembering an Earlier Case — and a Lesson in What's Unspoken

Back at the hotel, I thought about a case I had handled a decade prior. Two business partners. A factory. A rupture. And one painful insight:

It's rarely what's written in the contract. It's what was never said aloud.

That truth sat with me through the next morning.

Inside the Room — And Beyond the Blame

In our first session, each side spoke crisply:

Daniel: "You oversaw dismantling the machines. This is on you."

Alexei: "You chose the shipping company. You made the call."

They were both right — and both wrong.

I didn't argue. I simply asked:

"What happens if we do nothing? What is the cost of this pause? What's possible if we just move?"

I proposed a pivot:

Ship the equipment to Israel.

Let the original German manufacturer inspect.

Turn emotion into fact.

Silence.

Then: agreement.

What Was Repaired — And What Was Rebuilt

The following days were active: logistics arranged; procedures rewritten. But more than anything, the table between them — metaphorically — was rebuilt.

No winner. No grand payout.

But there was understanding.

On the Flight Home — A Note to Myself

Back on the redeye flight, I closed my eyes and scribbled a thought in my notebook:

"Sometimes, to make room at the table, you have to step back yourself."

Then another:

"In Rome, do as the Romans — but don't forget you're Israeli. And if your boldness comes with humility, maybe it's not audacity. Maybe it's a bridge."

This is the truth of Directed Mediation. It's not about neutralizing. It's about guiding — responsibly, humanely, with eyes open across language and legacy.

Sometimes, slowing down creates the only pace everyone can follow.

And often, what breaks the deal isn't what's said — but what remains unsaid.

CHAPTER EIGHTEEN

What Wasn't Written — And What Changed Everything

When a Contract Isn't Enough, and the Conflict Begins Where Silence Starts

Midway through a deal — that's often when the deepest fault lines begin to shake. Not a technical dispute. Not just a clause in need of rewriting. But something deeper: a small hole in the contract through which pain, disappointment, and betrayal pour.

It started with a phone call. On a day I had planned to disconnect from the world, the world called back. A long-time client. Familiar voice. Slightly strained.

"I don't know if it's already too late… but can you hear me out? It's not just the money. It's about what we understood — and what they now deny."

I knew exactly what he meant. Days later, I found myself in the mediation room. Two partners. Two expressions. A five-page agreement that seemed to cover everything — and yet, what it omitted turned out to be everything.

"It was always clear," said one — a seasoned entrepreneur. "We agreed to pitch to our investors first. This isn't about profit. It's about principle."

His partner, a lawyer by trade, replied evenly: "If it was so important, why didn't you write it down?"

And that was the start. Not of a technical review — but of a journey into what wasn't written, yet was felt as the very heart of the deal.

For the first few days, the mood remained procedural. Polite. Legalistic. But with each document produced, each email revisited, the emotional tide swelled.

"You forgot who brought you to this table," said the entrepreneur. "And you want me to sign off on something we never agreed to," replied the lawyer.

Still, they stayed. Not because they agreed — but because they wanted to know if anything could still be salvaged.

I asked them each to describe how it all began. The early partnership. The shared values that hadn't been drafted but had once defined their collaboration.

The entrepreneur recalled late-night drives, unspoken agreements, nods before key calls. The lawyer spoke of drafts, revisions, and footnotes.

"As long as I wrote it," the lawyer said, "it was real. But the moment I said something off-script — it vanished."

Silence.

That's when I stepped in. Not as a referee — but as a Directed Mediator. Someone who doesn't just ask questions but offers directions.

I proposed a hybrid model. A marketing approach that acknowledged the unwritten understanding, while staying within the bounds of the contract. Legacy investors would be offered first access to the bank, backed by a system of shared reporting and joint discretion.

There were no handshakes. No celebration. But for the first time, they looked each other in the eye.

As we finalized the amended agreement, I thought: some contracts could be written. Others are lived.

On my way home, their silent history reminded me of myself — back when I was a young attorney. I remembered waiting in a courthouse for a hearing, reading The Firm by John Grisham. One passage stuck with me — a young lawyer discovering the difference between what's in the document and what's believed:

"It's not about what's in the contract — it's about what you believe the contract means."

I had once made a verbal agreement that was never put to paper. When it all unraveled months later, I learned: what goes unsaid is often the first thing forgotten.

That's why I didn't let this one go. I fought — not for a clause, but for the right of the party who hadn't drafted the deal to feel seen, understood.

Sometimes, being a mediator isn't about reading what's there — but listening for what isn't.

Just before walking into my home, I stood under the evening sky, letting the day settle.

Not every partnership starts with words. But almost every fracture begins with a silence that was never given form.

And our role — as mediators — is to listen, not just to voices, but to what they couldn't say.

Because often, what wasn't written is the most powerful part of the story.

And if it's not on the page — it's our job to see it anyway.

CHAPTER NINETEEN

The One Who Steps In — And Dares to Stay

When the Mediator You Choose Changes Not Just the Deal, But the Journey Itself

They didn't want a judge.

Not a referee.

Not a familiar face from their past.

They asked for a mediator.

A certified one — someone who could "sit with them and figure out what's worth saving."

That's how the assistant phrased it when she called.

The call came on a Tuesday evening, just as I was wrapping up two exhausting days of back-to-back mediations. My mind was still lingering on the story of a young couple splitting their apartment before marriage.

What made me stop and listen wasn't the case, but the silence behind the request. That quiet hesitation in the caller's voice. The pause of someone who no longer knows how to move forward.

It reminded me of my own silence, from years ago, when I sat on the other side of the table. After I left the firm, I had built it. After the partners I once believed in walked away, leaving behind unanswered calls and open questions. Back then, I needed someone to sit with me and say, "There's still a way."

First Meeting: 26th Floor, behind a Closed Door

They waited in a glass room, high above Ramat Gan. Three partners, each with a lawyer. One looked hollow-eyed from fatigue. Another fidgeted restlessly with a pen. The third sat bolt upright, as if still performing for someone unseen.

The coffee was cold. The AC was too strong. The documents were already on the table before I introduced myself.

"We'll try mediation," one attorney said, "but you should understand — the gaps here are significant. My client has no intention of backing down."

I listened. And while he talked about gaps in numbers, I thought about another kind of gap — the way each man breathed differently.

One breathed with anger.

One with fear.

One like he'd already given up.

A Memory at the Red Light

On the way to that meeting, I stopped at a familiar red light near my old office. I remembered a time I turned down a similar case.

I didn't have the energy. I didn't want to deal with another bitter real estate dispute between partners who couldn't see past themselves. I told myself one of them might become a client later, not the right case.

So, the case went elsewhere. The mediator was professional but lacked real connection to the field. The mediation collapsed after two meetings. The project was sold for pennies. A waste.

That night, for the first time, I asked myself: "Do I always know when to say yes? Or when to stay?"

The Difference Between Certified and Right

In Directed Mediation, you don't just come with credentials. You come with the ability to read contracts and read between the lines.

To hear not just what parties say, but what they're afraid to say.

They weren't asking for a compromise.

They were asking if someone could walk through a minefield with them — and come out holding a map.

I introduced myself briefly. Not as a fixer. But as someone willing to walk with them.

Nobody smiled.

But I knew — there was a chance.

The Mediation Process: Silence, Fracture, Then Shift

The first session was procedural. Documents. Positions. Deadlines.

The second person. One-on-one.

That's when the truth emerged:

One had discovered that a partner's relative withdrew funds from a joint account.

They hadn't spoken for over a year — employees relayed messages.

None of them wanted the court. But no one wanted to be the one who looked weak.

The third session — a turning point.

Silence.

Twenty minutes in, Zvi looked at me and said:

"The problem isn't the split. It's that if I agree, it means I failed."

I told him:

"There's a difference between giving up — and choosing. Giving up means you're out of options. Choosing means you've seen the full picture."

Breaking the Ice

Then something unexpected happened.

The quiet partner slammed his hand on the table.

"Enough. Let's just sign. We're not kids. If you can't lead us, I'll walk."

I said, "No, you won't walk. We'll finish. But this time, by choice."

And in that moment, I was back in a room where I once had a similar conversation — when everything was falling apart, but someone — maybe me — chose to stay.

From Reality, Not from Law

In the days that followed, I drafted a deal based not just on law, but on reality:

- Distribution based on projected cash flow, not current valuation

- Mutual security guarantees for implementation

- Rolling compensation for one partner, paid over three years

• Mutual silence clause to protect reputations

When we signed, there were no embraces.

No smiles.

But one of them whispered at the door:

"If we'd gone to court — we'd have lost even what we had."

The Real Resolution

The resolution wasn't about land.

It wasn't about compensation.

It wasn't even about who was right.

The resolution was about who could guide them toward a resolution.

They were right to seek someone who was not just certified but aligned.

Maybe I'm not the best mediator in the world.

But I know what silence sounds like when it speaks louder than words.

I know what it's like to sit in a room and be afraid to go first.

I know what it feels like to start over, rebuild from zero, and not give up.

And I know that in the end, people don't remember the clauses.

They remember whether someone was truly there.

So, when you choose a mediator, remember:

A certificate is a requirement.

But the person is the real agreement.

Sometimes there's no time to think.

Everything falls apart.

And the heart must keep going — even when the site comes to a halt.

Postscript: A Late Night, a Book, and the Silent Hero

That night, long after they'd left and the agreement was signed, I found myself reaching for a book that had accompanied me through many sleepless nights: To Kill a Mockingbird. The part where Atticus Finch stands alone, defending what others won't touch, not because he expects to win, but because it's right.

It reminded me of something simple, yet powerful: Sometimes the role of a mediator isn't to solve the conflict. It's to stand—still, present, and steady—when no one else can.

And in that presence, a kind of peace emerges. Not legal peace. Not contractual certainty. But human peace. The one that lasts.

CHAPTER TWENTY

When the Site Stops — and the Heart Must Keep Going

How One Bold Solution Saved a Project from Collapse — When Everyone Else Gave Up

It wasn't just another morning. The phone rang before 8 a.m. No caller ID. No warning. Just a short vibration and a low voice, almost whispering:

"The construction stopped. We have a problem."

There was a long pause. I waited. A silence like that usually brings bad news, but this time I felt the weight before I even heard the details.

"Who are you?" I asked.

"I'm part of the tenant committee. We were referred by one of the lawyers. It's a large group. We're managing an urban renewal project — a mixed-use complex under a buyers' group. Final stage. Everything was nearly done. And then the contractor just... stopped showing up. The site is shut down. There's a lawsuit. There's pressure. And the bank—well, they're breathing down our necks."

I'm used to calls like this. But something about his tone—the caught breath, the urge to say everything without saying too much—put me on alert.

"I need everything," I told him. "Contracts, declarations, protocols. And if you can plan a contingency. Ten a.m. sharp."

A Full Room and Empty Faces

They entered the mediation room like survivors of a storm. Five tenant representatives. Confused. Angry. Exhausted.

They weren't developers. They were people with neighbors. With families. People entrusted with others' hopes.

One of them whispered, "My daughter goes to school with the contractor's son. I can't look him in the eye."

"Who signed the contract?" I asked.

Silence.

Then: "All of us."

In that moment, I didn't just hear the answer — I felt the burden. There was no clear villain here. No single person to blame. Only shared silence, shared shame, and shared responsibility.

Cracks Before Collapse

This was supposed to be a success story — an urban renewal project in the heart of Ramat Gan. Dozens of families. Evacuation and reconstruction. Bank financing. Cohesive buyers' group.

But the contractor, selected through a public tender, started slowing down. Delays. Missing reports. Unkept promises.

A demand letter. Then a disciplinary hearing. Then—nothing. The site was abandoned. Containers sealed. Workers vanished. The bank demanded clarity.

The first meeting? Chaos. Everyone spoke a different language: legal, technical, emotional. The trust—the lifeblood of the project—had evaporated.

I offered Directed Mediation. Not just listening. Leading. Deciding. Resolving.

They agreed.

Phase One: Who's Who and What's What

In the next 48 hours, I held separate sessions with:

- The tenants' committee

- The contractor's lawyers

- The supervising engineer

- The bank

- The project account manager

Documents piled up. Dozens of files. Reports. Emails. Minutes. But more than anything else, tension.

Everyone was waiting. And time was bleeding money.

Phase Two: The Weakest Link

The bank wanted certainty. The contractor wanted compensation. The residents wanted peace.

No one wanted to blink. Because blinking looked like weakness. And weakness had a price.

I needed a way where no one visibly lost—but everyone could move forward.

Personal Flashback: The Day My Office Went Silent

During one of the sessions, I had a flashback. A vivid one.

It was a year earlier. My law office — the one I had built from the ground up — had just been sold. Or so I thought.

The partners I had trusted chose another path. Left me with silence. Not betrayal — just a void. Questions unanswered. Phone calls not returned. Familiar faces are now unfamiliar.

That week, I sat in my own empty conference room, staring at chairs that once held dreams. I remembered asking myself: "Do I start over? Or do I stop altogether?"

That's the energy I brought into this room. That's why I knew what they needed.

Phase Three: A Solution in Real Time

Thursday, 9:00 a.m. White walls. A dry-erase board. One small room.

I put the proposal down:

- Immediate termination of the contractor — without admission of fault

- Partial release of guarantees — contingent on cooperation

- New contractor to be selected from a pre-approved bank list

- Six-month legal standstill — to stabilize the build

- Preservation of future legal rights — to avoid derailment

No one spoke.

Then, someone whispered:

"It's not perfect. But it's a hell of a lot better than where we are now."

Within Two Weeks

The project restarted.

The replacement contractor stepped in.

The bank gave the green light.

Residents were briefed.

The original contractor didn't return—but didn't disrupt either. His reputation was left intact. The gears began turning again.

Not because of a court.

Because someone decided.

What I Learned

Sometimes you don't resolve the dispute. You just keep it from wrecking everything else.

Sometimes there's no victory—just people who didn't lose themselves in the process.

Directed Mediation, in the moment, isn't a legal tool. It's a lifeline.

Because when everyone runs out of strength, sometimes all they need is silence, and one person who doesn't flinch.

The Only Thing They Wanted

No compensation.

Not a verdict.

Just a roof.

Just a key.

Just the right way to go home.

Epilogue: When Everything Stopped

I drove back from the mediation center late that night.

Silence in the car. No music. No phone calls.

Just headlights. And the sound of breath.

At a red light, I looked up and saw a billboard advertising a luxury project downtown — the same area where the site had just been resurrected.

I thought of all the people who passed it every day. Who never knew how close it had come to collapse.

And I smiled.

Because sometimes, the most important things don't make the news.

They just happen quietly — between people who refuse to give up.

That's what Directed Mediation is for.

And that's why I stayed.

CHAPTER TWENTY-ONE

The Time I Said Yes

When Humor, Friendship, and a Tangy Dispute Met at One Table

Some mediation cases begin with legal threats.

Others with silence.

This one began with a recipe — and a crack in the heart of a friendship.

It was a holiday. The kind where time slows down, and the city holds its breath between closures. I had promised myself a day of rest — no screens, no meetings, no stories to hold for others.

Then the call came.

From an old friend. The kind whose voice you recognize even before the second ring. The kind who knows not only your number, but your nature.

He got straight to the point:

"I've got two friends. They run a grill house together — small, popular, personal. They're fighting. Not over money. Over a sauce. I know it sounds silly. But it's not. It's gotten real. You're the only person I trust to help. Just hear them out. That's all."

I hesitated. Not because I didn't care. But because I'd just wrapped two intense mediations, I was still unpacking an emotional case from the week before, and honestly — I needed quiet.

But something about his voice — the blend of urgency and affection — got to me.

So, I said yes.

The Smell of Smoke and the Weight of Unspoken Words

The moment I walked in, I knew this wasn't about food.

The place smelled incredible — seared lamb, roasted tomatoes, and something smoky and warm. But the tension? It cut through the air like a knife through grilled meat.

One partner was behind the counter, polishing the same plate over and over. The other lingered near the kitchen door, arms folded, watching every move.

When they finally sat down, it wasn't with words. It was with silence.

"Do you even mediate over this kind of thing?" one of them asked.

I raised an eyebrow.

"Depends on what 'this kind of thing' really is."

The Real Recipe

Turns out, one of them had changed the signature sauce. Just a tweak — some tangy sweetness in place of the smokey heat.

The customers? Loved it. Reviews glowed. Sales bumped.

But his partner? Felt betrayed.

"He didn't ask. He didn't consult. He just did it. That's not how we work. That's not how we built this place."

What followed wasn't loud. It was sharp, but cold. Orders delayed. Ingredients questioned. Employees caught in the crossfire.

And underneath it all?

A friendship bruised.

A foundation shaken.

The restaurant was born from loyalty. One's wife had painted the signage. The other's cousin delivered the meat.

Now? They didn't even share eye contact.

Breaking Bread (and Tension)

I invited them to the corner booth. No papers. No laptops.

Just us. And some warm bread. And the story.

"Tell me about your first day. Tell me why you started this."

And they did.

The stories came out slow, then faster. The fryer fire on opening night. The regular couple who always ordered extra eggplant. The long nights. The victories.

Until we hit the wall.

"You changed the flavor," one said.

"You stopped showing up on Thursdays," the other replied.

There it was.

The sauce was just the symptom.

The illness was absent.

A Spicy Suggestion

I made a proposal.

Not a compromise.

An invitation.

"Put both kebabs on the menu. Let the customers decide. A taste test. One week. Winner stays."

They blinked.

Then laughed.

"A kebab contest?"

"Call it whatever you want. But let the food — and the people — speak."

One Week. Two Recipes. One Outcome.

They ran it.

Both sauces. Same kebab. Customers voted with tokens.

The result? A tie.

But something else happened.

They started laughing again.

Staff tension dropped.

And one night, they stayed late — just talking.

They kept both sauces.

Called them "His" and "Mine."

The tagline?

"Two flavors. One fire."

The Real Yes

I didn't say yes to a sauce.

I said yes to a friendship worth saving.

To a moment that might have passed if no one paused to catch it.

Sometimes, being a mediator means stepping into a story that looks small — but holds everything.

Pride.

Memory.

Fear.

And the quiet miracle of forgiveness.

This case didn't make the news.

But it stayed with me.

Because some of the most meaningful work we do — starts with a dish someone refused to change.

And ends with a table no one wants to leave.

Epilogue: A Taste That Lingers

A week after the vote, I returned to the restaurant. Not as a mediator. Just as someone hungry for a good story — and a better kebab.

The partners greeted me with smiles. Real ones this time.

The waiter brought out both kebabs. "His" and "Mine."

I took a bite of each. My eyes closed.

They tasted of cumin, lemon, fire — and something more.

Respect.

Restraint.

The flavor of hard-won peace.

And that's the taste I've come to crave most — the one that says: we were close to breaking but chose to break bread instead.

That's why I said yes. And why I still would.

CHAPTER TWENTY-TWO

One Presence That Changed Everything

When Presence Means More Than Words – And a Cultural Figure Quietly Resets the Tone in a High-Stakes Mediation

This chapter centers around a singular presence — a cultural guru, a revered rabbi, and a North American religious leader who had invested in a real estate project in Israel and became the silent key to resolving a public, escalating dispute with the local developer. Through both personal and professional lenses, the story explores how integrating figures of deep trust — even when not formal stakeholders — can transform an impasse into open dialogue.

The Meeting That Wasn't

It began in disappointment. Not mine — theirs. A long-planned meeting between myself and the negotiation team representing a religious investment group from North America was suddenly postponed, just two days before the scheduled date.

The message was brief:

"Until the rabbi gives his blessing, we don't gather."

This rabbi had no formal role in the project. He wasn't a shareholder. He hadn't signed any contracts. But he was the presence. Not a power by law — but by loyalty. He was beloved, trusted, a spiritual father who knew how to quiet storms before they erupted.

Only once it was confirmed that the rabbi would be visiting Israel for a family celebration did I receive another call. The door reopened. The mediation could proceed.

The Developer's Frustration

The Israeli developer, young, energetic, sharp, was infuriated.

"What does a rabbi have to do with a real estate dispute? This is about numbers, financing, and execution timelines. Why am I being asked to explain my schedule to a spiritual leader?"

I listened. Then I explained. About the nature of leadership in closed communities. About the pain they carried — not because the deal failed, but because it happened without his awareness. About the emotional contract that runs parallel to the legal one.

It didn't land right away. But slowly, he understood.

A Silent Entrance

Tuesday afternoon. The rabbi arrived. No speech. No blessing. Just presence.

He sat down gently. Then I asked one question:

"What broke the peace?"

Then he turned to me and said:

"I don't decide. But I trust you to uphold their dignity. Remember — not all truths are written into contracts."

And in that moment, I realized:

My role wasn't just to mediate between two parties. I was bridging worlds.

A Shift in the Room

From that moment, everything changed. The mood. The tone. The trust.

The meetings that followed were more open. The community members began to speak. The developer softened. The words used became less accusatory, more collaborative. Money, while still relevant, became just one of many factors.

By the time the agreement was finalized, the rabbi was already on his flight home. He didn't sign it. Didn't witness it. But his signature? It was in every line.

The Power of Presence

This mediation taught me something simple yet profound:

Sometimes you don't do the work. You just hold the space for it to be done.

You're the one who stays in the room so that trust can enter. So, the dialogue can begin. And so that someone who's never studied mediation — can give voice to a truth no one else dared speak.

Not all authority comes with a decree. Some come with quiet.

That's the role of a cultural guru — not to replace the mediator, but to empower them too truly mediate.

Other Echoes

Since that case, I've seen it time and time again.

In one story — told to me by a fellow mediator — it wasn't a rabbi but a Bedouin sheikh in Israel's south who shifted the conversation. The issue was land rights. No lawyer or government official could get past the silence. But the sheikh, with a lifetime of earned trust, unlocked movement without ever naming sides.

In another — a housing dispute in northern Israel — a beloved local council leader joined a meeting just "to be present." He said little. But his mere participation changed the energy. The deal signed that day bore his presence in spirit.

And not all of these figures are religious. Some are secular. Some are educators, financial mentors, retired generals. People whose integrity resonates beyond policy.

What Mediation Can Be

Mediation isn't one model. It's a flexible frame — a room large enough to invite in trust, nuance, and layered identities.

In deeply rooted conflicts — where culture, history, trauma, or mistrust sit just below the surface — there is power in asking:

"Who else needs to be here so people can start believing again?"

And Then Someone Stands Up

But what happens when the deal is drafted, the parties seem ready — and then someone stands up?

No signature. No closure.

Just a moment.

What do you do?

Sometimes, you bring back the presence.

Sometimes, the only way forward... is silence shared with someone who sees deeper than you can.

And as I remember that final look the rabbi gave me — not gratitude, not approval, but trust — I hear again the words:

"A human being is a bridge. But if it isn't poured right — everyone falls."

Sometimes, all we're called to do — is hold the mold while the concrete sets.

That's when mediation becomes something more. That's when we learn what silence, faith, and presence can build.

CHAPTER TWENTY-THREE

Everyone Said Yes – Then He Stood Up

When Mediation Was One Step Away from Closure – and One Person Shifted the Entire Equation

They sat around a brand-new, square table in a polished conference room I had rented specifically for this mediation. Everything was meticulously arranged – hot coffee, personalized notebooks, even sparkling water no one asked for. I wanted to convey a fresh start. Mediations of this kind – with serious money, sharp interests, and strong personalities – require a stage.

And not by coincidence, just before the meeting began, I remembered Amir. A good friend. One of those who remembers your name even when you forget who you are. In those hazy first months after I left my law firm – when everything felt uncertain – he was there. Not just with kind words, but with action: offering me his conference room, bringing a spare laptop from home, and setting up the very first client meeting of my new journey as an independent mediator.

Sometimes, you're on top – and then comes the fall. But if you know how to use it right, it becomes a launchpad.

They sat around the table. Nine men, two women, and I – a mediator who thought he'd seen everything. The documents were laid out.

The agreement was drafted. Every clause is reviewed, revised, and highlighted. The reading was quiet. Almost ceremonial. Then the signing began.

One by one – names, dates, weary smiles. And then, when we reached him – he didn't extend his hand. He raised his head, looked me in the eye, and said: "I'm not signing."

There was no drama. No anger. No outburst. Just a simple, quiet, painful truth. Like in a film, where everyone is convinced, we've reached the end – and the protagonist rewrites the final scene. "I'm sorry," he said. "I'm not sure this is the right thing."

Silence. Someone placed their pen down. A woman murmured, "But you said…"

He nodded. "I did. But I haven't signed."

It was a moment of truth. Like in 12 Angry Men. Not shouts, but silence. Not protest – but discomfort. That moment when one person, with one quiet decision, collapses the entire mechanism. He wasn't a lawyer. Not a power player. Just a person, with a doubt.

From that moment – we didn't speak about the agreement's content. We spoke about boundaries. About what constitutes true consent. About whether words are enough. And what happens when trust breaks just before the ink dries.

This man – he wasn't a saboteur. He wasn't trying to ruin anything. On the contrary: throughout the entire process, he had been involved, contributed ideas, acted responsibly. But suddenly, as the ink dried on the signature before him – he froze. Something in him hesitated.

Not for the first time in my life, I was reminded that mediation – like everything else – depends not only on what is said, but on when, how, and how the speaker feels.

He didn't want to wreck the deal. He wanted clarity. To pause. To think. And the system – designed to move forward – doesn't always know what to do when someone stands still.

So, we stopped.

Not a trial. Not a breakdown. Mediation. Pure and simple.

And I, in the center, thought about all those times in life when I said "yes" – but felt "no." How many times I smiled through negotiations, but wanted to scream. How many contracts I signed – only to lose sleep that night. Just like the day I signed the annex that cancelled my law firm partnership – not by real choice, but out of a forced sense of necessity.

That time, I wanted to yell "Stop!" – but I signed anyway.

This time – I had the privilege of being on the other side. Not pressing. Listening.

So we returned to the dialogue. Like jurors in a windowless room. We re-asked every question. Why this agreement? What does it truly serve? Where did compromise begin – and where did it become compromised of the self?

Three more weeks. No pressure. No manipulation. A new proposal has been drafted. Different in details – similar in essence. But with one major change: No one signed until their heart said yes.

And since then – I carry that moment with me.

Not to fear it – but to respect it. To remember that not every "yes" is a signature. Not every silence means agreement.

And sometimes, like in that film – it takes one person to say "no" for everyone to understand what truly matters.

And that – perhaps – is the biggest difference between litigation and mediation:

One seeks who's right. The other asks: Who's not ready?

And our role as mediators is to notice that moment – and tell the room: We're not done yet. Because unless you've truly signed with your heart – better not to sign at all.

But Why Do We Break Down at the End?

I've seen it before. Moments before completion – a hand trembles. A chair shift. The atmosphere, light just seconds ago, thickens like fog. And I ask myself: Is this fear? Is it grief? Is it the feeling of letting go of the fight — and with it, letting go of identity?

You see, conflict becomes part of you. It shapes your language, your sleep, your daily rhythm. People adjust to conflict. It becomes their reason to keep going. So, when a resolution arrives — it's not always liberation. Sometimes, it feels like a loss.

In that room, I watched someone struggle not with logic — but with release. He wasn't rejecting the proposal. He was grieving at the journey.

The Courage to Reopen

It takes bravery to break the momentum. To raise your voice — or your hand — and say: "I'm not there yet." Especially when everyone else is nodding. Especially when the table is set, and the deal is ripe. It feels like betrayal. Like weakness.

But what if it's the opposite? What if it's integrity?

That's what I saw in his eyes that day: not fear, but conscience. And as a mediator, I knew: my duty is not to finish. It's to finish right.

We Spoke Again

He shared his doubts. His history. A previous partnership gone wrong. A signature he regretted for years. A divorce was finalized too soon. Every page of this new agreement echoed pages from his past.

We spoke of fear. Of accountability. Of what a name on paper really means.

Others listened — not with judgment, but relief. Because his "no" gave them permission to re-evaluate, too. It opened the door to questions they hadn't dared ask. And from those questions — a better agreement was born.

Not Just a Deal – a Decision

The final agreement wasn't dramatically different. But the room was. People signed not from fatigue — but from clarity. And that makes all the difference.

What We Carry Forward

Since that day, I have built time for hesitation into every process. I allow for silence. I invite second thoughts. Because I've learned: that's where wisdom lives.

In one word: pause.

That's what we need more in this world — not faster results, but deeper consent.

And When You're the One Saying No

As for me — I carry my own unsaid "no." That day I signed a contract to walk away from a firm I built, a dream I carried. I said yes — with my pen. But no one asked my heart.

This chapter — this case — gave me back my voice. Not through victory. But through presence.

It taught me that every "no" deserves a room. And that one person's hesitation is not an obstacle. It's a compass.

Because sometimes, the person who stands up isn't stalling the end. He's starting the truth.

And so, as I left that room — empty of paper, but full of possibility — I knew:

The hardest yes, you'll ever say… is the one that comes after the no you dared to speak.

Next: What Happens When You Signed — and Regret It Right After?

Because not all journeys end at the signature line. Some begin the moment after. And that — as we'll explore — may be the real test of mediation.

CHAPTER TWENTY-FOUR

The Signature That Stopped the Clock

When a Mediator Is Asked to Decide — and One Voice Quietly Refuses to Follow the Script

I remember the night before.

Not because I was eager, but because I was uneasy.

I knew this case would be different.

And I knew exactly why.

Two parties.

One Israeli developer, sharp and strategic — Gadi.

One Jewish-American investor — David — a veteran of Wall Street,

and not a man to be rushed.

They had a contract.

They had a partnership.

They had a vision for a multi-million-dollar commercial center in northern Israel.

But somewhere along the timeline,

the numbers began to shift.

Deadlines blurred.

Tension built.

And eventually — the words became legal threats.

There was, however, one hope baked into the original agreement:

a mediation clause —

but not just any clause.

A Med-Arb structure.

Three sessions of mediation.

If no resolution was reached — the mediator would issue a decision.

Binding.

Final.

Enforceable.

They agreed to it.

Signed it.

Even joked about it in our first meeting:

"Like a friendly court — with coffee."

So, I got to work.

Session One: airing grievances.

Session Two: outlining positions.

And by Session Three —

I knew we wouldn't reach voluntary consensus.

I drafted my proposal.

Detailed.

Balanced.

Signed it with the authority they gave me —

as mediator, transitioning to arbitrator.

Gadi nodded.

David requested 48 hours.

He flew back to New York.

And then, the email arrived.

"I cannot accept the decision. I never agreed to arbitration."

Just like that.

The foundation cracked.

And I — the mediator entrusted to help them cross the river — was suddenly the bridge under fire.

David claimed he misunderstood.

He believed we were still in "discussion."

That nothing was binding.

That he'd been misled.

Gadi exploded.

"He agreed to the clause! We shook hands!"

And me?

I stood there — in the middle.

Watching a handshake unravel into accusation.

I went back.

Reviewed every document.

Every word from our first session.

The agreement was there.

The transition from mediation to decision was clear.

But clarity, I realized,

is not always comprehension.

The Human Behind the Signature

David was not I.

But he was overwhelmed.

Afraid of being boxed in.

Afraid that a process that began with conversation

had ended with judgment.

He didn't resist the logic of the proposal.

He resisted the speed.

The loss of control.

The silence after the decision.

It struck me deeply —

because I'd been there.

Not as a mediator.

As a man.

I had signed my own papers once —

ending my career as a firm owner.

Not from power.

But from fatigue.

Not because I was sure.

But because I was too tired to fight.

For weeks afterward,

I replied to the moment.

What if I'd paused?

Asked for another hour?

Another day?

Maybe nothing would've changed.

But maybe — everything.

That's what I saw in David.

Not betrayal.

But a man unsure of the silence he was walking into.

What I Did Next

I called him.

Not as a mediator.

As a person.

We didn't talk about clauses.

We talked about fear.

And regret.

And pace.

I didn't withdraw the decision.

But I delayed its effect.

I gave him — and Gadi —

a window.

A 7-day reflection clause.

An opportunity to submit any final concerns.

Gadi agreed.

David exhaled.

We moved forward.

Eventually, a different arbitrator was chosen.

My decision became background.

A foundation — but not a finish line.

And That's When I Rewrote the Rules

From that day on,

every Med-Arb clause I help with draft includes:

A recorded verbal explanation.

A cooling-off period.

A reaffirmation clause before any binding transition.

Because signatures without soul — don't last.

Because decisions without readiness — create resistance.

Because my job isn't just to write agreements.

It's to build bridges strong enough to carry people.

Even when the wind changes.

Transition to the Final Chapter

And sometimes,

it's not the terms that break the agreement.

It's what we bring into the room —

unspoken fears, personal grief, unresolved past.

In the next — and final — chapter,

I'll take you somewhere even deeper.

Not a boardroom.

Not a dispute.

A moment.

A personal one.

The moment I crossed to the other side.

A quiet ending.

A fierce beginning.

CHAPTER TWENTY-FIVE

The Edge of Resolution: When Letting Go Isn't Peaceful

"Sometimes, walking away isn't surrender. It's a strategy. It's the quiet decision to burn the bridge behind you — not because you're lost, but because you know you're never returning."

When I Became the Mediator

I made the decision.

Not out of weakness. Not out of fatigue.

But from clarity.

I chose to initiate a meeting—not through lawyers, not through formal letters, but personally. I would be the mediator in the most personal case of my life.

No attorneys. No buffers. No scripts.

Just the people who mattered, the conflict that tore us apart, and a chance—slim as it was—to put an end to it without losing what was left of ourselves.

I didn't expect it to feel this heavy. Not after everything I had already endured.

But when I sat down to draft that first message, offering to meet face-to-face, I knew I was stepping into fire without armor.

The silence after I sent it was long.

Too long.

Then, finally, a response.

A willingness to talk.

It didn't mean we were close to a resolution. It meant the door had opened. Barely.

Still, even a crack of light is enough for someone who remembers what darkness looks like.

We didn't have peace. We didn't have a date. We didn't even have trust.

But we had a room.

And sometimes, that's where revolutions begin.

And just like that, the battle changed shape.

It felt like dragging a corpse through a courtroom.

Act I: The Legal Wound That Wouldn't Close

I had already paid the price.

Not just the legal fees—those were incidental.

But the sleepless nights, the sense of injustice, the slow erosion of trust.

They took what I built.

Tarnished what I stood for.

Filed motions with language that cut like glass—

each paragraph meant to reduce me to a version of myself I didn't recognize.

And I fought back.

With documents. With declarations.

With the full weight of my truth.

But truth doesn't pay interest.

It doesn't rebuild a reputation.

And the lawsuit—as righteous as it felt—was eating away at something more precious than justice.

It was costing me my focus.

The Mediator's Dilemma — This Time, With Skin in the Game

I teach others to settle.

To listen.

To lead people through their most painful compromises.

But nothing prepared me for this.

To mediate your own wound is to reopen it.

To stand in the middle and say:

"I'll be the adult in the room,"

even when the child inside you wants revenge.

So, I didn't say yes. Not immediately.

Instead, I said: "Send me their draft. I'll read it."

What arrived wasn't an offer. It was a gamble. A calculated proposal that offered closure, at a cost I wasn't sure I could live with.

And just to be clear — we haven't signed yet.

Not as of the time I'm writing this.

We're still circling, trading drafts, wording clauses like chess moves.

But I know where this is going.

And the direction alone speaks louder than any verdict could.

This isn't surrender. It's the opposite.

It's the belief that I can rebuild from scratch —

not despite what happened, but because of it.

That I can choose to walk away,

not because I lost,

but because I finally remembered who I am without the noise.

The Proposal: A Peace That Doesn't Heal

They offered to withdraw the counterclaims.

To cancel the future payments.

To never speak of the dispute again.

No apology.

No acknowledgment.

Just silence — bought and paid for.

In return, I would waive everything.

All rights.

All claims.

All sense that I was right and they were wrong.

It was legal.

It was efficient.

And it felt like swallowing glass.

Speaking to the Ghosts of My Integrity

I took a walk that night.

Past the office where we first started the firm.

Past the building where I had once signed my name under theirs—

believing we were building something that would last.

But legacy is fragile.

Not because of what others do,

but because of what we choose to carry forward.

And I realized:

I wasn't trying to win anymore.

I was trying to be heard.

And sometimes, the only way to be heard

is to say nothing.

To walk away—not because you're weak,

but because you're the only one strong enough to end it.

I kept hearing the same sentence in my head:

"You're a mediator now. Act like it."

Only this time, I was mediating for someone I had never really met before:

myself.

The Meeting Before the End

No one arranged this meeting for me. No attorney paved the way. I made the call. I chose the room. I set the tone.

Not after dozens of mediations. Not after years of resolving other people's wars. This time, it was mine — and I stepped into it not as a lawyer, not as a claimant, but as a mediator of my own conflict.

I wasn't posturing. I wasn't bargaining. I was trying to speak a language no one else in the room remembered — the language of resolve.

We sat at the table. No judge. No press. No advocates whispering in our ears.

Just three people who had once shared an office —

now divided by lawyers, silence, and the residue of everything left unsaid.

I read the agreement. Word by word. Word by word. Each clause felt like a stitch over a wound that had stopped bleeding — but never healed.

And then I said something no one expected:

"I'll sign. But not because I forgive.

Because I'm done."

They didn't answer.

They just nodded.

The Signature That Wasn't a Surrender — Yet

I almost signed up.

The agreement was on the table. The terms agreed. The principles — aligned. It should have taken hours. It's taking days.

Because now, new parties have entered the scene. Stakeholders with opinions. Voices with agendas.

And suddenly, what felt like a precise act of closure has started unraveling.

What happens when the mediator leaves the room?

Everyone talks louder. No one listens.

What was once a shared space for resolution becomes a battlefield for positioning. Each person protecting their corner of influence. Each side pulling the fabric back to their advantage.

And I'm watching it happen.

Knowing exactly what's going on.

Knowing exactly what's being missed.

But the irony?

The one who led them to this moment isn't being heard now.

Not truly.

And still — I hold.

I wait.

Because I know that every deal worth signing must pass through fire first.

And if it comes — the moment, the pen, the page —

it won't be surrender.

It will be the last act of courage in a room that forgot who brought the courage in.

The Fire That Still Burns

People ask me why I'm even considering settling.

Why, after all this — after taking a stand, after building the case, after exposing the truth — would I even entertain the idea of closing this chapter with a signature rather than a verdict?

I give them the same answer:

Because this story was never about the court.

It was about the real cost — the emotional toll, the years of strain, the personal trust eroded through endless battles. It was about reclaiming belief in myself, and choosing to spend my time on what builds, not what breaks.

And no judgment could ever restore the time, the spirit, or the clarity that was taken.

No — we haven't signed yet.

Not as of writing these words.

We're still in it. Still revising.

Still watching as new voices enter the room and dilute the truth with noise.

But the decision to initiate that meeting — to mediate alone — was the turning point.

Because I chose to stop waiting for someone else to do what I already knew how to do.

And if I could do that — in the one case that shook everything I am

Then maybe I've earned the right to call myself a mediator.

Not because I succeeded.

But because I didn't run.

I was stuck in the fire. And I spoke.

Not for the case.

For the future.

And that's what makes this chapter worth telling — even if the ink isn't dry yet.

Why didn't I take them to the end? I give them the same answer every time:

"I didn't settle. I chose to begin."

The lawsuit may be over.

But the story isn't.

Because now, I know what it means to let go —

without peace.

And I keep walking.

And if I could do that — in the one case that touched everything I am —

Then maybe I finally earned the right to call myself a mediator.

Not just for others.

But for myself.

FINAL CHAPTER

When You Cross to the Other Side:

A Quiet Ending. A Fierce Beginning.

This is not just the end of a book. It's the opening scene of the next chapter. Not as a lawyer. Not even as a mediator. But as a man standing in the fire of his own conflict.

For years, I walked into rooms as a composed one. The listener. The observer. The one who guided others through their turmoil without becoming consumed by it.

But this time? This time, the fire was mine.

I left behind a thriving law firm.

Not out of failure. Not from exhaustion. But because I saw something bigger — something I needed to build.

A method. A mission. A new way to lead.

Not through hesitation — but through clarity. Not by waiting for endless consensus — but by offering precision and presence.

I didn't walk away to vanish.

I walked away to begin.

But every new beginning comes at a cost.

And then — the letter.

No phone call. No meeting.

Just ink. Cold, surgical, impersonal.

"We are offsetting the agreed sum."

It wasn't the money.

It was the betrayal.

Of loyalty. Of trust. Of history.

So, I did what no one expected: I filed a lawsuit. Not in anger. But with resolve. Because silence here would've meant surrender.

Every word was deliberate. Every sentence, a calculated defense. Not to harm — but to protect what mattered.

They thought I wouldn't fight. Because I meditate. Because I listen. But listening isn't a weakness. And mediation — when done right — is the fiercest form of standing.

There are many kinds of battles.

Some are loud.

Some are quiet.

This one? It was calculated. Relentless. Personal.

Because the hardest battle is the one you never asked for.

The one you did everything to avoid. And still — it comes.

I enter mediation rooms every day.

I give everything I have.

To people I've never met. To stories that aren't mine.

Because I believe in resolution.

Because I believe in peace.

But then I walked away from this room.

And I remember:

I am in conflict too.

Uninvited. Unwarranted. But real.

And that's what distinguishes a method from a life. Because when the mediator becomes the case, every silence, every glance, every hesitation… carries weight.

You begin to see things differently.

Not as roles.

But as wounds. As choices. As truths.

This isn't about revenge.

It never was.

It's about reclaiming who you are — when others try to erase you from your own story.

Because they wrote: "We are offsetting."

But I?

I am not something you can subtract.

You cannot take a man's name away.

You cannot negotiate his dignity.

This is not a signature at the bottom of a contract.

It's a declaration.

I believe in mediation.

But I also believe in justice.

And the two must always coexist.

So if this book ends here — know that I do not.

I step into every room now, carrying both:

The silence I honored.

And the voice I reclaimed.

Because some stories don't end with peace. They end with truth. And some truths are not heard. They are lived.

This is mine.

And it stays.

Forever.

Afterword: What Comes Next

Every ending begins something new.
This book was written about real rooms.
Real silences.
Real people.

Sometimes the moments were broken.
Sometimes they were brave.
But always — they were human.

Mediation isn't magic.
It's not a trick. Not a script.
It's a choice:
To listen.
To understand.
To decide.

When I crossed to the other side of the table,
it wasn't just a moment of crisis —
it was a moment of clarity.

I had to mediate not just for others,
but within myself:
between past and future,
between loss and creation.

If you've made it this far,
perhaps something in you stirred, too.

This book wasn't written to instruct.
It was written to connect.

And if it touched you — even for a moment —
then it has done what it came here to do.

From here, I move forward.
To guide.
To mediate.
To write.

Because between silence and decision,
there is still truth to uncover —
and stories yet to be told.

— A. Lalum

Decision-Oriented Mediation

1. Core Principles

A structured approach to resolving complex disputes with clarity, presence, and accountability.

2. Structured Process

Every mediation begins with a clear roadmap — expectations, goals, and timeframes. Clarity leads to focus. Structure invites trust.

3. Deep Listening

Before any decision can be made, the mediator listens deeply: To what is said. To what is left unsaid. To what silence dares to reveal.

4. Professional Presence

The mediator is not neutral in action — but neutral in intent.

They stand steady — offering direction when chaos rises, holding space when others can't.

5. Proposal and Timing

The right proposal isn't just what is said — but when.

Timing is often the true turning point.

6. Decision — When Needed

If consensus fails, the mediator may offer a clear, balanced recommendation. Where pre-agreed, even a binding resolution. Because sometimes, resolution requires responsibility.

7. Respecting the Human Element

Behind every clause stands a person — with fears, memories, and hope.

No process is complete without honoring their truth.

This model wasn't written in theory.

It was born in rooms where people weren't just stuck — they were breaking. Where they needed more than words.

They needed direction.

"Between silence and decision, there is a space where resolution lives —and I choose to work there."

– A. Lalum

www.ingramcontent.com/pod-product-compliance
Lightning Source LLC
Chambersburg PA
CBHW060947050426
42337CB00052B/1622